Landscapes of
ANDALUCIA
Costa del Sol and sierras

a countryside guide
Sixth edition

John and Christine Oldfield
revised by *Sunflower* Books

SUNFLOWER BOOKS

Sixth edition
Copyright © 2024
Sunflower Books™
P O Box 36160
London SW7 3WS, UK

All rights reserved.
No part of this publication may be reproduced, stored in a retrieval system, or transmitted by any form or by any means, electronic, mechanical, photocopying, recording or otherwise, without the prior written permission of the publishers.

Sunflower Books and 'Landscapes' are Registered Trademarks.

ISBN 978-1-85691-557-1

Important note to the reader

We have tried to ensure that the descriptions and maps in this book are error-free at press date. It is very helpful for us to receive your comments (sent to info@sunflowerbooks.co.uk, please) for the updating of future printings.

We also rely on those who use this book — especially walkers — to take along a good supply of common sense when they explore. Conditions change fairly rapidly in Andalucía, and ***storm damage or bulldozing may make a route unsafe at any time***. If the route is not as we outline it here, and your way ahead is not secure, return to the point of departure. ***Never attempt to complete a tour or walk under hazardous conditions!*** Please read carefully the Country code on pages 7-8, the Walking notes on pages 47-52, and the introductory comments at the beginning of each tour and walk (regarding road conditions, equipment, grade, distances and time, etc). Explore *safely*, while at the same time respecting the beauty of the countryside.

Cover photograph: the Caminto del Rey (Car tour 4, Walk 14)
Title page: typical in all Andalusian pueblos blancos *in autumn is the wrought-iron balcony hung with* pimientos *(red peppers) set out to dry.*

First, Second and Third editions by John and Christine Oldfield. All later editions revised by Sunflower Books.
Photographs: pages 30 (bottom), 33, 36-7, 38-9, 109, 118 (bottom): iStockphoto; pages 43, 70, 136, 140: Paranga Images; pages 22-3, 25, 54-5, 64, 92, 103, 108-9 and cover: Shutterstock; all other photographs: John Oldfield
Maps: Nick Hill for Sunflower Books. Base map data © OpenStreetMap contributors. Contour data made available under ODbL (opendatacommons.org/licenses/odbl/1.0)
A CIP catalogue record for this book is available from the British Library.
Printed and bound in the UK: Short Run Press, Exeter

Contents

Preface	5
Nature notes	6
Country code for walkers, motorists and picnickers	7
Language/Glossary	8
Picnics and short walks	9
Touring	14
THE ALPUJARRA (Tour 1)	16

Almuñécar • Órgiva • Pampaneira • Bubión • Capileira • Pitres • Pórtugos • Trevélez • Vélez de Benaudalla • Almuñécar

   SIERRA NEVADA (Tour 2) — 21

Almuñécar • (Detour 1: Canal de la Espartera) • (Detour 2: Sierra Nevada Visitor Centre • Maitena Visitor Centre) • Granada: the Alhambra • Armilla • Jayena • Otívar • Jete • Almuñécar

   THE AXARQUIA (Tour 3) — 27

Cueva de Nerja • Frigiliana • Cómpeta • Canillas de Albaida • Salares • Canillas de Aceituno • Puente Don Manuel • Vélez Málaga • Torre del Mar • Torrox Costa • Cueva de Nerja

   ANTEQUERA AND THE LAKES (Tour 4) — 32

Torremolinos • Parque Natural Torcal de Antequera • (Antequera) • El Chorro Nature Reserve • Carratraca • Torremolinos

   SIERRA DE MIJAS (Tour 5) — 35

Benalmádena Costa • Mijas • Puerto de los Pescadores • Fuengirola • Benalmádena Costa

   SIERRA DE LAS NIEVES (Tour 6) — 38

Marbella • (Istán) • San Pedro • Ronda • El Burgo • Guaro • Monda • Ojén • Marbella

   SIERRA DE GRAZALEMA (Tour 7) — 43

Ronda • Villaluenga del Rosario • Benaocaz • Ubrique • El Bosque • Benamahoma • Puerto del Boyar • Grazalema • Ronda

Walking (● see explanation of symbols on pages 47-48)

Grading, waymarking, maps, GPS	47
Where to stay	49
Getting about	49
Weather	49
What to take	51
Potential hazards	52
Organisation of the walks	52

4   Landscapes of Andalucía

WALKS IN THE ALPUJARRA
- 1 Busquístar • Baños de Panjuila • Ferreirola • Atalbéitar • Busquístar   53
- 2 Capileira: the three bridges   57
- 3 Río Naute, below Mulhacén   60
- 4 Three Andalusian villages: Capileira, Bubión and Pampaneira   66
- 5 Pampaneira • Soportújar • Carataunas • Órgiva   68

WALKS IN THE SIERRA NEVADA
- 6 Vereda de la Estrella (Pathway to the Star)   71
- 7 Collado de las Sabinas   75
- 8 Toma del Canal   77
- 9 Boca de la Pesca   81

WALKS IN THE AXARQUIA
- 11 Cueva de Nerja • La Civila • Cortijo Molinero • Cueva de Nerja   85
- 11 Camí de las Cabras (Ibex Trail)   90
- 12 Fábrica de la Luz and Cueva de Melero   94
- 13 Alcaucín Valley: Ventas de Zafarraya to Puente Don Manuel   96

WALK IN EL CHORRO NATURAL PARK
- 14 Three walks in El Chorro Natural Park   101

WALKS IN THE SIERRA DE MIJAS
- 15 Ruta Cruz de la Misión   105
- 16 Pico Mijas   108

WALKS IN THE SIERRA DE LAS NIEVES
- 17 Marbella • Puerto de Marbella • Olivar de Juanar • El Cerezal • Ojén   111
- 18 Istán   115
- 19 Río del Burgo   119
- 20 Peñón de los Enamorados (Lovers' Rock)   123

WALKS IN THE SIERRA DE GRAZALEMA
- 21 Grazalema • Merendero del Boyar • Llano de las Presillas • Llano del Endrinal • Grazalema   128
- 22 Benaocaz • Casa del Dornajo • Puerto de Don Fernando • Salto del Cabrero • Benaocaz   133
- 23 Río Majaceite   139

Bus and train timetables   141
Index (of geographical names)   143
Touring map/plan of Marbella   *inside back cover*

Below: The Vega de Granada, with the snow-capped peak of Cerro de Caballo (3013) in the distance (Car tour 2).

 Preface

Despite only covering about a third of Andalucía, this book still takes in a huge area and is intended as an introduction to the south-central part of the region. The carefully chosen tours and walks fan out from the Costa del Sol — east to Granada and the Sierra Nevada, and west to Ronda and the Sierra de Grazalema. When you return (as you surely will!), you will find ample material on the ground to explore more intensively the landscapes that most appeal to you.

EU investment in decades past helped Andalucía to flourish. As a visitor, you will appreciate the fairly speedy travel time between the main centres, thanks to the many new *autovías*. But some of the *pueblos blancos* suffered, and are no longer quite the stuff of picture postcards: anywhere within striking distance of the coast, hillsides are peppered with residential complexes and villas. But the historic centres of these little 'white villages' have managed to retain their tranquil charm — and these settlements are still gateways to breathtakingly beautiful mountain and valley walks.

For ten years after this book was first published, the authors made frequent trips to Spain, and were fortunate to meet many 'Landscapers' using the book and recounting their experiences. Now that John and Christine Oldfield live too far away to continue revising the text, Sunflower hopes you will keep your written comments coming, to help our updaters in the field. Apart from these necessary revisions (changes of road numbering, timetables, waymarking, closure of walking routes and the like), Sunflower has made no other editorial changes, since the love of Andalucía's landscapes shines through every page of John and Christine's original text.

SUNFLOWER

Nature notes

As you travel through this area of Spain, and read our text, there are certain natural features which will frequently catch your attention. Some are explained below.

Alcornoque Cork oak tree, abundant throughout Andalucía. Its wood, hard and resistant, is fashioned into barrels and tools, and its acorns are used for animal feed. But principally it provides cork. Once stripped of the cork bark, contact with the sun turns the yellowish-coloured trunk a vivid red for a while — spectacular to behold, but not touched unless you fancy stained fingers.

Algarrobo Carob or locust tree. Common on many of the walks, its presence is usually announced by heaps of fallen pods around the base of the trunk. Large and brown and sometimes called St John's bread, the pods contain a sweet nutritious pulp said to be the honey eaten by St John the Baptist. The fruit is used in the preparation of a chocolate substitute and the seeds are supposed to have been the origin of the carat weight.

Cabra montés Translates literally as mountain goat but is actually the Spanish ibex, with characteristic long straight horns (see photo on page 86). Small herds roam the Andalusian mountains, particularly in the Parque Natural Sierra de las Nieves, where fences and grids keep them from straying off the hillsides. Look for them silhouetted majestically against the skyline or springing nimbly across the slopes. Most likely to be spotted or heard around November, the rutting season, when they are frolicsome.

Cañada Gully or ravine, recognized in the past as a drove road or right of way for animals. Often clearly marked on Spanish topographical maps by a double dotted line and looking invitingly like a good track. Herdsmen may once have moved their livestock along these *cañadas*, but few of them are suitable for walkers.

Pinsapo *Abies pinsapo Boiss*, the Spanish fir (sometimes known as hedgehog fir), a tree whose dark blue-green branches sprout huge bright green buds in spring. Over the centuries numbers have declined, and it is now confined solely to the mountains of Andalucía, particularly within the natural parks of the Nieves and

Pinsapos *in the Cañada del Cuerno (Walk 20)*

Grazalema sierras. Ancient and majestic, it is variously referred to as the jewel, the king or the emblem of the natural parks — and deservedly so.

Vultures The Parque Natural de la Sierra de Grazalema supports the largest breeding colony of griffon vultures in Europe. They are gregarious birds and you will see groups soaring and circling above as you drive or walk in the park. The black vulture, an endangered species, is present in much smaller numbers and is usually seen solitary or in pairs. One of the world's largest birds, with a wingspan of almost 3m, it is a sight to remember.

Country code for walkers, motorists and picnickers

The Spanish countryside is essentially unspoiled. Only around the more accessible, and therefore popular, picnic or camping areas is there a litter problem. Please do not be tempted to add to it. Fire is a major hazard in countryside that is always parched in summer and, of late, all year round. Respect the country code and ensure that this beautiful area remains unspoiled.

- **Do not light fires.**
- **Protect all wild or cultivated plants.** Don't pick wild-flowers. Never cross cultivated land and do not be tempted to pick fruits, almonds or olives as these are clearly someone's private property.

- **Do not disturb or frighten animals or birds.**
- **Keep to designated paths.** Erosion is a problem in many mountain areas, and much of it is caused by overzealous walkers taking short-cuts.
- **Walk quietly through farms and hamlets.**
- **Take all your litter away with you.**
- **Protect water sources.** *Fuentes* (springs) in the mountains are especially important. When attending to 'calls of nature' keep well away from springs and streams and make sure that you bury all paper.
- **Walkers — do not take risks!** *Never walk alone* and *always* tell someone where you are going and when you expect to return. It might be helpful also to leave this information on a note in your hotel room and/or in your parked car. Any route could become dangerous after storms. If you are lost or injured you may have to wait a long time for help.

Language/Glossary

Many people on the tourist beat speak English, but since that is not the case in the villages, a simple Spanish phrase book or phone app can be invaluable. It is useful to know some of the common Spanish words which crop up frequently in a countryside context. Some of them appear in the text *(in italics)*, and you will rapidly become familiar with them. They are listed in the glossary below, along with some other words that you may encounter on your travels.

acequia narrow water channel
algarrobo carob tree
alcornoque cork oak
arroyo stream
autopista motorway
autovía expressway
ayuntamiento town hall
baño bath
barranco gorge, ravine or gully, usually dry
bocadillo sandwich
búho owl
burro donkey
cabra montés Spanish ibex
calle street
camino 'way' (a small street, track or path)
cantera quarry
cañada gully, ravine or right of way
carretera main road
casa/casita house/little house
casa consistorial town hall
cerro hill
collado mountain pass or saddle
correos post office
cortijo Andalusian farmhouse
coto privado de caza private hunting reserve
cueva cave
embalse reservoir
era threshing floor
ermita chapel, shrine
finca farmhouse and farm
fuente spring
gasoleo diesel
gasolina petrol
hostal cheap hotel
junta council
lavadero wash-house
merendero snack bar/country restaurant
mirador viewpoint
molino mill
nieve snow
parque park
peñón rock
pinsapo Spanish fir
playa beach
plaza square
puerto mountain pass or sea port
refugio mountain hut
río river
seco dry
toro bull
torre watchtower
vega plain
venta roadside restaurant
zona recreativa official picnic area/facilities

Picnics and short walks

In contrast to many other parts of Spain, there seem to be few official picnic areas in Andalucía. Those we found, designated by ⏶ in the text and on the maps, are generally attractive and well laid out, but very busy at weekends and *fiestas*. But who *needs* benches and bins? It's not too difficult to find secluded and spectacular alternatives. All the information you need to locate some of our favourite spots is detailed below. *Picnic numbers correspond to walk numbers* (except those at the end of the list, prefixed 'CT', which are specific to a car tour). You can quickly find their general location by looking at the maps where the location of each picnic site is indicated by the symbol P. Remember when you park your car never to block a road or track.

Although one or two of the sites are close to the road, others involve an interesting short walk, and sometimes some ascent or descent. Be sure to read the full description and equip yourself with all you might need, for example stout walking shoes, sunhat, suncream and ground sheet. You will sometimes have access to a *fuente*, but do not rely on this as your only water supply.

Most of our chosen spots are close to rivers, streams or reservoirs, and many enjoy spectacular mountain views. Nature lovers will delight in the fresh air, the variety of trees and shrubs, the abundance of wildflowers and the company of birds, both great and small.

All picnickers should observe the country code on pages 7-8.

1a Old mill at Busquístar (map on page 55)

⏶ to Busquístar (Car tour 1); 20min on foot. Follow Walk 1 as far as the river bed (❶). Picnic by the water in this picturesque spot. There is shade if you want it and a lovely ambience.

1b Baños de Panjuila (map on page 55)

⏶ to Cortijos de Panjuila (Car tour 1); 13min on foot. Follow Walk 1 from ❸ down to the *baños* at ❹. Fill water bottles from the *fuente* and sit on the rocks or in the shade just beyond the ruins, water cascading below and a panorama of brilliantly-white villages dotted all over the hillside.

3 Puente Abuchite (photo on page 57, map on page 59)

⏶ to Capileira (Car tour 1); 25min descent on foot. Follow Walk 3 as far as the bridge over the Poqueira River (❷). A marvellous setting, in a deep gorge, with shady trees, fast-flowing clear water and rocks to sit on.

6 Estación de San Juán (map on pages 72-73)

🚗 to the 46.2km-point on Detour 2 of Car tour 2; 56min on foot — or no walking if you drive along the narrow tramway route to the old station. Follow Short walk 6, or else walk along the tramway in both directions. This wild spot at the end of the tramway (❷) offers a fast-flowing river, pools, steep rocks and cliffs, shade or sun as you wish and the opportunity to potter about by the waterside in a wonderful setting.

7 Ruta de las Sábinas (map on page 76)

🚗 to the 38km-point on Detour 2 of Car tour 2; 11 or 16min walking. Park off the road at the bend and take the track going to the right, following Walk 7.
(a) At 11min, at a junction, take the middle track which rises slightly to a small, charming cabin, Cabaña Frasquita de Las Puentes. It is used as a weekend retreat but not signed as private. When no one is there it is a lovely spot with shade, a bench, and lots of atmosphere amongst the pines.
(b) At 16min there is a lookout spot at a 'balcony' above a house (❶). No shade but far-reaching views up the valley to the fantastic Sierra Nevada ridge.

8 Puente de los Siete Ojos (map on pages 78-79)

🚗 to the 11.7km-point on Detour 1 of Car tour 2; 25min on foot. Follow Alternative walk 8 from the 15min-point (the car park) to the 40min-point. This tranquil spot at the Bridge of the Seven Eyes (❹) offers views of Cerro Gordo rising on one side and Trevenque towering majestically above the other. An *acequia* starts nearby and a convenient flat area, shaded by trees, overlooks the clear flowing river.

11 Frigiliana falls (map on pages 88-89)

🚌 to Frigiliana (Timetable 5) or 🚗 to the 9km point of Car tour 3; 12min walking, with a *steep descent*. Follow Walk 11 upstream to the waterfall or choose one of several wonderful spots en route. Little shade.

12 Fábrica de la Luz (map on pages 94-95) 🍽

🚗 to the old church of Santa Ana in Canillas de Albaida (Car tour 3); no walking. Follow directions to get to the start of Walk 12. Choose your spot at this well laid out zona recreativa, with picnic benches, shade and toilets. Enjoy the sound of a flowing stream, stunning mountain scenery and midweek tranquillity. Why not take a stroll upstream — just follow Walk 12 as far as you like.

14 Mirador de los Embalses (map on page 100)

🚗 to the 113.5km-point of Car tour 4. Park at the Restaurante el Mirador; 13min on foot. Follow Walk 14-A to the *mirador* (❷). Sit on the rocks at the top of the cliff, overlooking the magnificent El Chorro gorge. You may be lucky enough to share your view with the vultures that patrol the cliffs. Surrounding pines provide shade if needed.

15 Ermita del Calvario (map on page 106, photo on pages 36-37)

🚌 or 🚗 to Mijas (Car tour 5); 16min on foot, on a steep but easy zigzag path. Follow Walk 15 up to the *ermita* (❷). There's a bench in full sun on the little patio or you can sit on rocks on the surrounding slopes, where you will find some shade from pines. Encircled by the Sierra de Mijas, you have magnificent and far-reaching views over the village and agricultural land to the coast.

17a Finca Manzah Al Kaid (map on page 112)

🚌 or 🚗 to Marbella (Car tour 6); 16-19min on foot. Follow Walk 17 to the 16min-point. Picnic in the open area by the waterside (❶) or go a little further upstream to an even nicer spot, surrounded by mountains and with fresh running water and shady trees— but stop short of the line of beehives. After rain you'll need a ground sheet.

17b Mirador de Juanar (map on page 112)

🚗 to the gate, just past the entrance to the Refugio de Juanar (see Short walk 17 on page 111); 35min on foot. Follow the Short walk to the *mirador* (❻; limited shade, rocks to sit on, views all the way to the coast).

18a El Nacimiento (map on page 115, photo on page 118)

🚌 (infrequent) or 🚗 to Istán (a detour on Car tour 6); 15min on foot. Follow Walk 18 to the 15min-point at ❶, where water cascades down into pools by the side of the quiet road. Low walls to sit on, a little shade and, after rains, a tumbling waterfall.

18b Mirador de la Herriza II (map on page 115)

🚌 (infrequent) or 🚗 to Istán (a detour on Car tour 6); 36min on foot if you follow Short walk 18 to ❹; 9min on foot if you walk there straight from the car park (Short walk 18 in reverse). There is no shade, but there are stone benches with superb views to the glistening reservoir.

19a Río del Burgo (map on pages 120-121, photo on page 41)

🚗 to El Burgo (Car tour 6); 31-38min on foot. Follow Walk 19 to the 31min-point (❶; above the weir). Picnic here in full sun on the rocky promontory, or go down the chained-off track to the waterside in the shade of trees. Have a paddle or even a bathe and enjoy the tranquillity.

19b La Fuensanta (map on pages 120-121) 🛐

🚗 to the Fuensanta track just south of El Burgo (Car tour 6); 36min on foot — or no walking at all if you drive along the track. If you avoid weekends, you may well have this enchanting picnic/camping area to yourself (❽) — apart from the woodpeckers. Benches are set in woodland on the banks of the Arroyo de la Fuensanta, where a restored mill provides a picturesque focal point. A shrine to the Virgen de las Nieves adorns its entrance, and a courtyard boasts toilets, showers, and a *fuente* with four spouts.

21 Puerto del Boyar (map on pages 130-131)

🚗 to the *merendero*, just beyond Puerto del Boyar (Car tour 7); no walking or a 10min climb requiring stout footwear. Go through the gate to the left of the *merendero* (❶) and sit on the concrete walls by the water (if any), source of the Río Guadalete. Or, preferably, continue by following Walk 21 from the 45min-point up to the level grassy area and choose your spot among the shady pines overlooking the valley. There are rocks to sit on, a backdrop of rugged cliffs and a spectacular outlook over the Puerto — definitely worth the climb.

22 Arroyo del Pajaruco (map on pages 132-133)

🚗 to Benaocaz (Car tour 7); 24min on foot from the church. Follow Short walk 2 down the cobbled trail to the bridge (**9**). Sit on rocks by the waterside with trees providing shade. A convoy of donkeys, loaded with milk churns, passes this way several times a day on its way to and from a *cortijo* where the goats are milked.

23 Río Majaceite (map on page 139, photo on page 46)

🚗 to Benamahoma (follow notes on page 139 to get to Walk 23); up to 14min on foot. Follow Walk 23 for as long as you like. There are numerous attractive and secluded spots — especially the area around the second ruined mill (**2**), where there is open space, shady trees, flowing water, grass and rocks. You'll be entertained by the song and flight of lively birds and, if you're *really* lucky, you might see an otter.

CT1a La Poza (on the touring map and the map on page 59)

🚗 to Pampaneira. Park in the public car park; 15min on foot. Walk down from the main square to the road above the electricity station which comes into sight below. Turn right on a rough path/track which follows the Río Poqueira upstream. Mostly wide, with just a few narrow sections, it undulates above spectacular falls and pools to an attractive bridge and a dam. Known as La Poza, this former official picnic site was ravaged by floods. But it is still a lovely spot, with a flowing river, a *fuente*, grass and rocks to sit on, poplars providing a bit of shade and views down the valley.

CT1b The roof of Spain (on the touring map)

🚗 to Capileira. Take the optional drive up the Sierra Nevada road to the track; 6min on foot. Walk along the track until it opens out on the right to a gently sloping area of grass and rocks with low trees which provide limited shade. From this high vantage point views are absolutely stunning. Veleta (3398m) dominates the Sierra Nevada ridge, covered with snow until around April, while the coastal sierras line up below like a geographical model. Three villages, sparkling in the sunshine, complete the awe-inspiring picture.

CT1c Fuente Agria (on the touring map) 🍽

🚗 to just beyond Pórtugos; no walking. A pretty site with an *ermita* and mineral springs. Sit on the benches or by the stream; mature trees provide shade.

CT1d Trevélez (on the touring map; photo on page 19)

🚗 to Trevélez; no walking or up to 15min on foot. Park near the bridge and picnic by the river. Spots in the open close to the bridge may be busy; for a more secluded picnic, take the little path that goes upstream on the west side of the bridge. Should this be fenced off, walk into the church square and take Calle de la Cuesta; just behind the church, turn right on a wide track down to the river. Sun, shade and rock pools.

CT2 Embalse de los Bermejales (on the touring map)
🚗 to the 128km point; no walking. Sit among the pines, with the reservoir shimmering before you, then take a stroll along the water's edge.

CT3a La Rahige (on the touring map) ⊼
🚗 to the 66.8km point; no walking. This picnic/camping spot, set on shady slopes just alongside the road, is in wild countryside in the middle of nowhere and almost deserted during the week. Choose a secluded bench or sit by the side of the river near a little waterfall.

CT3b Embalse de Viñuela (on the touring map) ⊼
🚗 to the 86.7km point; no walking, but plenty of opportunity for a stroll above the reservoir. There are picnic benches and barbecues, and you can choose sun or shade in this glorious and spacious setting on the wooded banks of the *embalse*.

CT4 El Torcal (on the touring map, photo at the right)
🚗 to the 63.2km point; 2 to 30min walking. Follow the green-waymarked trail. You are spoiled for choice of picnic site in this *parque natural*, but one of the best is in an open meadow about halfway round the trail. Dwarfed by towering rocky sculptures (which provide adequate shade) and carpetted with delicate wildflowers, this is a wonderland of images. Scan the skies and you may spot griffon vultures soaring overhead.

CT6 Parque Natural Sierra de las Nieves: Conejeras (on the touring map)
🚗 to the 47km point. Drive for 2km along the good track to the Conejeras notice board by a stream bed; no walking. Sit on rocks and enjoy the wildness of this place. Limited shade, but spectacular surroundings — and a short walking trail on offer.

The green-waymarked walk at El Torcal ('Ruta Verde', Picnic CT4)

Touring

Andalucía is a vast region. You could spend a lifetime investigating the architectural and historical legacy of its chequered past and another lifetime exploring its mountains and river valleys. A few car tours can scarcely do it justice, but we have tried to ensure that you see the most representative features and experience at first-hand the vital and vibrant nature of this land.

Car tour 7 starts from Ronda, but all the others start from the coast and can easily be picked up at intermediate points if you wish. Apart from the main north to south arteries, roads through the mountains are narrow and winding. Take great care, always expecting the *unexpected*. Heavy storms can cause sudden and considerable damage, leading to diversions and delay. Thank heavens that **road numbering** seems to have settled down; the numbers on our map and in the notes are correct at press date, but some may change again…

You will derive little pleasure from the tours if you rush from place to place trying to pack in as much as possible in a short time. So, if possible, **allow a full day for each tour**, to ensure plenty of time to stop and explore as the fancy takes you. The scenery is so breathtaking that it should be savoured at leisure. Allow plenty of time, too, for the deservedly famous tourist attractions like the Cueva de Nerja, the Alhambra in Granada and Ronda's spectacular Tajo Gorge. And while the little white villages dotted all over the mountainsides are enchanting, you will have to park and go on foot to visit them: *don't* attempt to drive through their concreted narrow streets! Try to make time on each tour to do at least one of the short walks that we suggest and look out for the starting points of the longer walks, perhaps to be tackled another day.

Our touring notes are brief; we give only the minimum of historical or other information that you can find in standard guides or free tourist office leaflets. Instead we place emphasis on times and distances, road conditions and possibilities for sightseeing, **picnicking** and **walking**. The driving times assume driving always within the speed limit, but do *not* allow for any stops. Beware: short distances can often take much longer than expected.

The pull-out touring map is designed to be held out opposite the touring notes; the **symbols** in the map key correspond to those in the text. There are plenty of **petrol stations** on the main roads, but fewer in the mountains. They are always well signposted and usually open during normal business hours.

When touring always **carry plenty of water**. Although all the towns and some of the villages you will pass through have bars, they are not necessarily just where you need them. Bars that don't provide full meals usually have a selection of *tapas* or can make up a sandwich *(bocadillo)*, but it's really much better to plan on picnicking in the fresh air at one of the spots we suggest. Bars and petrol stations are likely to have **toilets** (and **telephones**, if your mobile battery is low).

Much of your touring will be at high altitude, and the air will be chilly even outside winter. Take **warm clothing** so that you can leave your car in comfort. Whatever the time of year, the sun can be strong, so **suncream and head covering** are essential if you intend to walk around.

Before you set off, *do* read the **Nature notes** on pages 6-7 and skim over the **Glossary** on page 8. And **please observe the Country code on pages 7-8.**

Church at Pampaneira, from the village wash-house (Car tour 1, Walks 4, 5)

Car tour 1: THE ALPUJARRA

Almuñécar • Órgiva • Pampaneira • Bubión • Capileira • Pitres • Pórtugos • Trevélez • Vélez de Benaudalla • Almuñécar

173km/107mi; 4h-4h30min driving
On route: ⛽ at Capileira, Fuente Agria; Picnics (see *P* symbol and pages 9-13): 1a, 1b, 3, CT1a-d; Walks 1-5

The Alpujarra, an exquisite area of mountains and river valleys, extends from the south face of the Sierra Nevada all the way to the Mediterranean. It was the last stronghold of the Moors in Andalucía, and many traces of their occupation still remain today. It is here that you will find the best examples of Berber architecture. Whitewashed houses, built in layers, each have a flat roof and distinctive chimney. *Tinaos*, or galleries, provide passage from house to house and between levels, and walls and balconies are festooned with colourful flowers in equally colourful pots. The Moors also developed a formidable system of *acequias* (water channels) to irrigate the land, and some are still in use today in market gardens and orchards. The Alpujarra is a botanist's dream, reputed to boast the highest number of unique species of flora in the world. Discover some of these for yourself by following the walks referred to in this tour.

From the roundabout by the bus station in **Almuñécar** (⛽🏨🛏🍴☕⊕) follow the N340 (signposted to Motril) east along the coast. This is a heavily built-up route, but hills rise quite close to the road on the landward side and in places steep cliffs drop down to the sea. Every so often their line is broken by delightful little coves and watchtowers *(torres)* standing sentinel above. The road winds across deep *barrancos,* with views of long-abandoned terracing on the slopes. You'll gasp as the small town of Salobreña comes into sight, built around the skirts of its ancient castle. In times past, the castle was used as a royal summer residence and also as a prison. Below, stretching towards the sea, is a fertile plain where sugar cane and cumin used to be the main crops. Pass the exit for Salobreña★ (12km ⛽🏨🛏🍴) — worth a visit, perhaps another day. Cross the plain and join the N323/GR14 to Granada (15km). If there is any snow lying on the high peaks of the Sierra Nevada, you will soon catch sight of it as the road heads directly towards the mountains, past fields of soft fruit, bananas and flowers. Ignoring the *autovía*, pass a petrol station (19km ⛽) and follow the wide Río Guadalfeo, a main fluvial artery of the Alpujarra, through a spectacular gorge. Shortly after another petrol station (25km ⛽) you will see the rectangular Moorish tower of Vélez de Benaudalla ahead.

At 30km, almost immediately after the road crosses the river, turn right across a bridge, following signposting to Vélez Benaudalla (A346). (The road continuing straight on goes to Granada; Car tour 2.) You are now on a narrower and winding road, with the river still on your left. A reservoir, the **Presa de Rules**, can

16

Bayacas is one of the little villages encountered on Walk 5, close to Órgiva.

be seen below (📷) as you drive high above the river, with cliffs on the right. Eventually Órgiva comes into view, tucked in at the foot of the high peaks. Turn left on the A348 (42.6km), cross the river on the bridge known locally as the Puente de los Siete Ojos ('Bridge of the Seven Eyes'), and reach **Órgiva★** (44km ⛽🏨✕🚌⊕△). This town, at a height of 450m, is considered the capital of the Western Alpujarra and has great historic associations. The church, with impressive twin bell towers (shown on page 70), dates from 1580 and is on the site of an old mosque. The valley around Órgiva is home to majestic olive trees, hundreds of years old, their trunks contorted with the passage of time.

Drive through the town and follow the road as it turns sharp left before the church. Just before the bridge, you pass a roundabout (45.4km), finishing point for Walk 5 which meanders down old trails from Pampaneira. At the next junction (46km 🚌) turn right towards Carataunas and Trevélez (A4132). This minor road winds up steadily into the Alpujarra, providing magnificent views across mountains and valleys and the numerous little white settlements dotted around the slopes.

Cross a bridge over the Río Chico and ignore the turn to Carataunas (52km ✕), which is visited on Walk 5. At 54.5km you pass the **Ermita del Padre Eterno**; it stands on a bend, at a junction where a forestry road climbs up into the Sierra Nevada. Summits visible from around here will be snow-covered for much of the year, and the altitude ensures that some bright pink almond blossom lingers well into March.

Two villages come into sight, then another, higher up on the slopes ahead. The three of them, overlooking the Poqueira Valley and shining brilliant white against the hillside, are typical of the region. Cross the bridge over the Río Poqueira and, just beyond the electricity station (59km), notice a track going uphill to the left: it eventually leads along the river to La Poza (map on page 67; *P*CT1a). Not far ahead is the first of the villages, **Pampaneira** (60km ⛽🏨✕M; photo on page 15), where Walk 4 comes in on an ancient trail from the next two villages on our route. Pampaneira is also the starting point for Walk 5. On coming to a junction (62km 🚌) turn left on the A4129, to drive through **Bubión★** (⛽🏨✕🚌) and reach **Capileira★** (67km ⛽🏨✕📷M). This village, shown on pages 58 and 64, is a popular walking centre. In putting together Walks 2, 3 and 4, all of which start here, we have tried to capture the best features of the

18   Landscapes of Andalucía

surrounding area. Short walk 3, to a delightful picnic spot by the riverside (*P*3), will give you a tantalizing taste, while Walk 3 is an exhilarating trek to the slopes of Mulhacén (photograph pages 62-63).

Possible detour: The main tour turns back from Capileira, but you might like to make a short (8km return) detour along the road ahead. This route eventually deteriorates to a track which climbs across the high peaks of the Sierra Nevada to the ski centre (we approach the ski centre from the other side on Detour 2 in Car tour 2). The central section of this track across the high peaks is now only open to walkers and cyclists, but if you have time it's worth driving the first part of it to enjoy the panoramic views. From the car park at the top of the village (❶ on the walking map on page 66; 🅿) continue up the steep winding road (Walk 4 follows this route, but turns down to Bubión after 0.8km). Park 4km uphill, at the point where there is a mirador and a motorable track (which goes to Trevélez) turns off to the right; the junction is signed with a red and white GR marker on a post. Why not walk a short way along the track (*P*CT1b)?

The main tour continues from Capileira: we retrace our route through Bubión and turn left at the junction on the A4132 (72km). After passing a *mirador* (📷), drive round the head of the valley at Barranco de la Sangre and climb gradually past the right turn to Mecina (75km). Drive through **Pitres** (77km ▲🅇△) and continue up into **Pórtugos** (79km ▲🅇🅿). A mulberry plantation was started here for the silk trade in the first half of the 20th century, and this industry thrived for some time. Just after leaving this town behind, you come to Fuente Agria (✝🅿*P*CT1c), mineral springs dating back to 1872. The five spouts are to be found just to the left of the pretty *ermita*, and people swear that the water gushing from each spout has different mineral properties. We're not sure about that, but can vouch for the fact that it all tastes quite bitter!

Continue to a fork at the entrance to **Busquístar** (81km ✝▲🅇; photo pages 54-55) and take the left-hand road signposted to Trevélez. To the right, the village itself is the start and end point of Walk 1 which leads to a lovely riverside picnic spot (*P*1a). As the mountains draw closer, you enter the Parque Natural Sierra Nevada. Then Trevélez comes into view, nestling in the valley with a snowy backdrop for much of the year. At 85km, on a bend, don't miss the Barranco de los Alísos, a good spot for a break. A path, overgrown in places, but colourful in spring and affording tremendous mountain views, goes up to the left, just before the bridge, and leads to waterfalls and a pool.

Follow the Río Trevélez upstream, through countryside which looks especially magnificent in autumn. Descend into **Trevélez★** (91km ▲🅇△), the highest settlement on the peninsula (1476m) and famous for its trout and *jamón serrano*, cured ham. Drive through the village overlooked by the magnificent peak of Peñabon and pause as you reach the head of the valley (*P*CT1d; photo opposite).

Having crossed the bridge,

look back across the river to Mulhacén, at 3482m continental Spain's highest peak. Notice, too, the chestnut trees along this spectacular route as the road now runs downriver, high above the water. At a crest (98.5km) turn right for Torvizcón on the A4130. Just before passing some distinctive rock formations, there is a helipad on the right: like the others placed strategically around the countryside, it is for use in case of fire or other emergency. You pass a series of old ruined buildings looking like barracks (102km) and probably associated with the mines nearby, then keep right at a junction signposted to Almegíjar. Walk 1 comes up from the valley on the track by the *cortijo* on the corner, follows this road for a short way, before turning off at the little hamlet known as **Cortijos**

Picnic CT1d: many people picnic near the bridge at Trevélez, but there are more secluded spots a short way upriver, where this photo was taken.

Acequia Baja, with Mulhacén in the background (Walk 3, detour route)

de Panjuila (103km). Stretch your legs here by following a section of Walk 1 to another choice spot for a break (*P*1b).

After noting some disused mines over on the left, bear right at the next junction for Almegíjar. Descend a little and pass the road to this village (108km), looking in spring for the tall asphodels growing along the verges. The road zigzags down into the valley, crossing the Río Guadalfeo again at 112km. Go right at the junction (114km) signed to **Torvizcón**, which you pass through at 115km (▲✕🍴).

Descend gradually, eventually rounding the head of a *barranco*, above Puerto del Juviley, set in a deep gorge forged out over centuries by the waters raging down from the Sierra Nevada. Beyond another helipad on the right, we reach the valley floor. Ignore the right turn to Órgiva before a tunnel (130km) and retrace a short section of your outward route, passing the Presa de Rules. Don't cross the bridge (142km): instead turn left and drive through the long main street of **Vélez de Benaudalla** (144km ✝▲✕). You might like to stop and look at the beautiful garden created during the 13th-century Nazarí dynasty. Central to its theme is water. At the very end of the village, take the narrow unsigned road from the roundabout which forks downhill to the right over a speed bump/zebra crossing. Turn left on the N323 and then right when you reach the coastal N340, back to Almuñécar (173km).

Car tour 2: SIERRA NEVADA

Almuñécar • Granada: the Alhambra • Armilla • Jayena • Otívar • Jete • Almuñécar

Without detours: 185km/115mi; 4h-5h driving; Detour 1: 23km/14mi, 40min driving; Detour 2: 63km/39mi, 2h driving

On route: ♁ at La Zubia, Sierra Nevada Visitor Centre; Picnics (see P symbol and pages 9-13): 6, 7a, 7b, 8, CT2; Walks 6-9

No visit to Andalucía would be complete without taking in one of Spain's most famous cities and setting eyes on the long curved ridge of the Sierra Nevada which boasts the highest peak on the Iberian Peninsula, Mulhacén (3482m/11,420ft). This tour enables you to do just that, and the two **highly recommended** detours lead you to walks right in the heart of the mountains. Snow lies on the peaks for ten months of the year but, lower down, especially in spring, the slopes are carpeted with wildflowers, many endemic to the Sierra Nevada region. You may wish to spend time exploring the historic sights of Granada, content to gaze upon the high peaks of the Sierra Nevada from thirty kilometres away. Or perhaps you will feel drawn to walk in these imposing mountains. To fit in both will require more than just one day, so do some planning before setting off. Whatever you decide, it will be an unforgettable experience. The tour is particularly enjoyable in early spring, when there is still snow on the slopes and the weather is warm enough to be comfortable when you venture out of the car. Avoid Sundays and holidays when the roads, particularly on the detours, will be very busy.

Follow Car tour 1 out of **Almuñécar** (✝♨⛰✕☕⊕) as far as the bridge across the Río Guadalfeo (30km). Instead of taking the slip road signed to Granada (GR14), go straight ahead until you can take the GR16 to Granada about 4km further on. This road bypasses all the industrial towns and permits a fast smooth ride. En route you can't fail to spot the wind farm (33km); the road becomes the A44 *autovía* shortly before passing the road to Lanjarón and Órgiva (41km), finishing point for Walk 5 which comes down from Pampaneira. Catch your first glimpse of the **Vega de Granada** (48km), the vast, fertile and undulating agricultural plain shown on pages 4-5. The road undulates as it climbs steadily but gradually to a pass, the **Puerto del Suspiro del Moro** (66km). From up here, the peaks of the Sierra Nevada are magnificent, even in summer when the snows have melted. Further on, you will see Granada spread out ahead. Keep following Granada, now on the G30.

Take exit 16 (75km) for the Alhambra and the Sierra Nevada; this is the 'Ronda Sur' (southern ring road). *If you are going to take Detour 1 (page 23), take Exit 2 off the ronda (76km), signposted to La Zubia.* Otherwise continue to follow the Alhambra signs into a two-lane tunnel. *If you are going to take Detour 2 (page 24), keep to the*

22　Landscapes of Andalucía

right-hand lane now. For the main tour take the left lane and follow magenta 'Alhambra' signs from the roundabout at the end of the tunnel. You find yourself climbing a hill, with fantastic views over the valley. Pass the coach park and reach the **Alhambra**★ (81km 🏛).

After your visit, turn back, so that you are driving towards the Sierra Nevada peaks. To explore Granada itself, turn right at the first junction ('Centro'). Otherwise, start the leisurely drive back to base, returning through the tunnel lane signposted to Jaén (87km). But very quickly take Exit 1c and stay in the left-hand lane for Ogíjares. Do *not* go left for Ogíjares at the roundabout; go straight over for Armilla. Keep following **Armilla** or 'Centro Ciudad' (✖) over various roundabouts until you get to a 'Stop' sign/traffic lights at a T-junction with the A338 (a little over 4km from Exit 1c). Turn left, passing an old disused airport on the left at once. Go through **Las Gabias** (94km ♣✖🅿) and continue across the plain. For as far as the eye can see there are green fields and neat rows of trees — mainly olives, but with some almonds among them. Pass a shooting centre on the right (98km) and wind steeply downhill with far-reaching views over terrain which is now much drier. Pass through **Malaha** (103km), a spa town with mineral springs. Its river is now virtually dry, all the water being diverted through a sophisticated irrigation system developed by the Arabs and still ensuring the agricultural success of the area.

You cross this section of plain on a long straight road, passing an industrial park (112km 🅿) just beyond the road to Escúzar. Climb into the low hills at the edge of the plain and pass through the little village of **Agrón** (117km). Then descend (121km), with views over the Almijara ridge and then the Embalse de los Bermejales below. At a junction with the GR3307, turn left for Jayena and wind downhill through almond groves, towards the reservoir. A track (126km) leads to the waterside, where you could picnic on the high banks or take a stroll through the trees (*P*CT2).

Continue to the southern end of the reservoir, pass a turning to Fornes, and drive on through the winding streets of **Jayena** (133km), now on the GR3302. After leaving this village and

Right: the Alhambra

Car tour 2: Sierra Nevada 23

crossing the Río Granada (134km 🍽), the road undulates through olive groves. The road is little used — not surprising, since it does not appear on some maps. At a junction (144km) turn right on the A4050 (signed to Almuñécar) and pass a restaurant (145km ✖). The Almijara ridge extends impressively on the right, and the road passes another restaurant (✖) and a turn to a 'Granja Escuela' (Farm School; 152km).

Then suddenly — and completely unexpectedly — the landscape changes totally. Rounding a bend, the road starts contouring around steep cliffs and through a pass 1.2km long. The scenery is breathtaking and awe-inspiring, a sort of moonscape with rugged hills and deep valleys. But keep your eyes on the road as well: it is narrow and winding, and cars sometimes take the curves on the wrong side. Views become even more amazing as each bend unfolds. To the right is the Sierra de Almijara and, to the left, the Sierra del Chaparral. At the end of the pass you come 'back down to earth' (158km) and head through gentler terrain (160km 📷). Not far beyond this lonely *mirador* there is a *fuente* on the left with clear cold water straight from the mountains.

As the road continues to wind, you may see notices asking you to sound your horn on the bends. You cross a bridge at the head of the valley. Notice Lentejí, a village high above, and drive through **Otívar** (172km ✖). The

surrounding slopes are dark and heavily wooded, mainly with pines, *nísperos* (medlars) and *chirimoyas* (custard apples). The Río Verde comes into view on the right (📷), and you follow it all the way to the coast, crossing it once.

Drive through **Jete** (176km) where there is a chapel in the rock dedicated to the Virgin of the Waters, pass a petrol station (179km ⛽) and, on the extreme outskirts of Almuñécar, reach signs inviting you to visit a fine Roman aqueduct★ (181km 🏛). It is definitely worth a stop and a leg-stretch, so park and take the steps which descend from the road. Then continue on into Almuñécar, arriving back at the roundabout at the bus station after 185km.

Detour 1: Ronda Sur • La Zubia • Fuente del Hervidero • Canal de la Espartera • Ronda Sur

From the Ronda Sur take Exit 2 (the 76km-point of the main tour) for **La Zubia** (⛰✕) and drive across the plain into this small town. Pick up green signs for 'Cumbres Verdes' towards the end of the town. Keep left at a mini roundabout and after 125 metres go right. This is the Huenes Valley road, and it climbs steadily through pine forests where picnic benches (🪑) sit amongst the trees. After passing the **Cumbres Verdes** housing development (⛰✕), the road loses its tarmac but is easy to drive.

Pine forests give way to open hill slopes and a turn-off to the **Fuente del Hervidero**, an isolated restaurant sitting amidst cultivated fields (10km ✕). Walks 8 and 9, both magnificent hikes, start from here. Why not take a half-hour break and enjoy some mountain air? Just park under the tree by the *fuente* and follow Walk 8 (page 77) to the 15min-point, where you will have the tremendous view shown opposite. Or *drive* to the viewpoint by following the rest of the detour, but *beware of potholes!* From here the road bears left and, shortly afterwards, on a sharp left-hand bend, you'll spot a track rising to the right, to a parking area at the **Collado de Sevilla** (11.7km). Whether you have come on foot or by car, you now enjoy fantastic views of the Alayos de Dílar, the crags overlooking the Dílar gorge. The rocky peak to the left of the crags is Trevenque (2079m), while just in front of you is an enclosed section of the **Canal de la Espartera**, an incredible feat of engineering which Walk 8 follows to its source. Short walk 8 continues along the dirt road to the Puente de los Siete Ojos ('Bridge of the Seven Eyes'; *P*8) set directly below Trevenque; Alternative walk 8 goes on from the bridge to get acquainted with the mountain from even closer quarters. To the right here are two buildings, one old and incomplete, the other a modern chalet, and a little lower down is the old Cortijo Sevilla. They make quite a picture with the Boca de la Pesca ('Fish-Mouth'; Walk 9) rising behind them.

Return to your car, wherever you left it, and drive back the way you came, enjoying even better views of Granada from this perspective. Turn right at the main road in La Zubia and drive out of the town and back onto the Ronda Sur at the roundabout (23km). Take the first exit, signposted to the Alhambra and Sierra Nevada. In the tunnel, take the left lane for the Alhambra and pick up the main tour again where you left it,

Right: Prado Llano (Flat Pastures), the ski village

or, for the second detour, take the right lane, signposted Sierra Nevada, which exits the Ronda Sur at the far end of the tunnel.

Detour 2: Ronda Sur • Sierra Nevada Visitor Centre • Prado Llano (ski village) • Güéjar Sierra • Alhambra approach road

Note: If you are not confident driving on rough, steep and narrow mountain roads with sheer drops to one side, plan to retrace your route from the Visitor Centre (37km), rather than completing the circuit.

Take the right-hand lane through the tunnel at the 76km-point on the main tour and find yourself on the main Sierra Nevada road (A395) leading to the ski village. Ignore exits to various small towns and villages and wind high above the valleys. This good road was built in 1996 for the World Alpine Ski Championships. For a while the surroundings are well cultivated with olives and almonds, but as the altitude increases these groves give way to slopes that are either barren or covered in pines. There are several restaurants and hotels (▲ ✕) on the route, and from the **Mirador del Embalse de Canales** (also called Mirador de los Enamorados; 14km 📷) you can appreciate the wonderfully exotic scenery. Down in the valley on the left lies a reservoir, the Embalse de Canales. You will soon begin to see vestiges of snow on the higher slopes (18.5km ⛽). Then, on a right hand bend, at a junction with the old road (19km), you come to El Dornajo, the **Sierra Nevada Visitor Centre** (*i*) at a place known as El Desvío. Walk 7 starts near here and you will return to this point after visiting the ski village.

Continuing uphill, after rounding a bend (22km) you come face to face — during most of the year — with snow-clad mountains. The ski village soon comes into sight at the head of the valley, and the ski slopes on Veleta (3398m) are clearly visible. We run out of superlatives when attempting to describe the exhilarating scenery up here — you *must* see it for yourself! A *mirador* (📷) with a *fuente* (24km) allows you to stop and take it all in. Then you reach **Prado Llano**, the ski village (28km ▲ ✕), at an altitude of 2075m. There is a huge car park (paid parking and no caravans allowed). This enormous purpose-built village is quite tastefully arranged around central pedestrian areas with shops, restaurants, bars and the ski schools and ticket offices. The residential buildings are piled in layers high up the hillside. It is worth exploring and getting good close-ups of the snowy slopes.

Leave the village (on the Granada road) and return to the Visitor Centre (37km). If you have decided *not* to follow the entire detour route, you can go straight back along the Granada road from here and rejoin the main tour at the 79km-point. (But if you would like to see the settings for Picnics 7a and 7b, you can carry on the further 1km with no problem.)

If you are game to carry on, leave the main road and drive up to the right, past the Visitor Centre; then fork left following signposting to the Seminario Sierra Nevada. Descend past several pine plantations and notice the village Güéjar Sierra across the valley to the left. As the road makes a hairpin bend to the left (38km), Walk 7 starts off on a track to the right.

Some 1.5km further on, on a hairpin bend to the left, go straight ahead on a narrower road signed to the Seminario and Hotel del Duque. Continue descending through pines and orchards, their blossom painting a colourful picture in early spring. The road soon becomes rough and potholed in places (40km), as you drive alongside some metal fencing and pass a *fuente* on the right and a left turn to the seminary and hotel. Ignore a track to the right as the road hairpins to the left (42.3km) and you pass below the hotel. With sheer drops to the right and no improvement in the surface, the road now zigzags steeply downhill — *take great care*. Reach a *cortijo* (44km), with particularly resplendent blossom in March. A little further down you pass the green entry gate to the *cortijo* and keep zigzagging down to the Mesón Restaurante El Charcón on the banks of the Río Genil (44.6km ✕).

There are a few other buildings on the banks of the river, and the route of an old tramway runs along the far side. The old tram used to carry people from the bustle of Granada to the Estación de San Juan, where they could enjoy a day out in spectacular countryside — a journey of some 20km, with a gain of almost 500m in altitude.

Cross the bridge over the Río Genil and bear left. Go through two tunnels and, after crossing the Río Maitena, fork right at the next junction, where the Restaurante Maitena lies to the left (46.2km ✕). It's housed in the old Maitena tram station. Walk 6 sets off from here and initially follows the tramline past the old Estación de Charcón, to where the fast-flowing Río Genil and surrounding rugged cliffs offer a dramatic picnic spot (**P**6) at the Estación de San Juan, where the tramline ended. The walk then continues upriver on the Vereda de la Estrella (Pathway to the Star); photos on page 74) for unforgettable views of the Sierra Nevada ridge.

Climb steeply, high above the valley, to a *mirador* (👁) with extensive views over the Genil Valley and the long thin Embalse de Canales. On reaching the large village of **Güéjar Sierra** (48km ⓘ✕) follow the one-way system in a sharp left turn, signposted for Granada. As you leave the village, now on a proper road, notice the amazing pinnacles towering over on the left. Continue past orchards and the village of Pinos Genil, high above the reservoir. Turn right for Granada (56.7km; signposted) and drive along a pleasant tree-lined road. At the next major junction (59.1km), go straight ahead through **Lancha de Cenes**. Fork right for the Alhambra (63km) and pick up the main tour at about the 80km-point.

Car tour 3: THE AXARQUIA

Cueva de Nerja • Frigiliana • Cómpeta • Canillas de Albaida • Salares • Canillas de Aceituno • Puente Don Manuel • Vélez Málaga • Torre del Mar • Torrox Costa • Cueva de Nerja

128km/79mi; 3h-4h driving
On route: ⊟ at La Rahige, Embalse de Viñuela; Picnics (see *P* symbol and pages 9-13): 12, CT3a-b; Walks 10-13

This varied and interesting tour circles the part of the province of Málaga referred to as the Axarquía, from the arabic word for 'eastern zone'. Sheltered from the cold and the winds by the Sierras de Tejeda y Almijara, it enjoys a balmy climate which the Arabs exploited by introducing sugar cane and wine and initiating the agricultural traditions of the area. As a result, trading prospered, with export of goods such as silk, raisins, figs, almonds, oil, wine and sugar. Tall chimneys of the many old sugar mills can still be seen today. In this rural environment, do not be surprised to meet flocks of sheep and goats on the road. On the circuit you will notice, from different angles, a village perched on top of a hill. This 'balcón de la Axarquía' is Comares, which boasts a 16th-century church and the ruins of its ancient castle.

Start the tour from the **Cueva de Nerja★**, just north of the N340, close to Maro. This vast cave, discovered by children in 1959, is one of the most beautiful in Europe. Nerja made news headlines in 2012 when six paintings of seals were discovered in the complex. They are believed to be 42,000 years old — the oldest artwork in the world, predating by 10,000 years cave paintings in southwest France attributed to Homo Sapiens. The Nerja paintings could only have been created by Neanderthals, which would radically alter our understanding of Neanderthal man.

Walk 10 starts here at Nerja and climbs high into the mountains, while the short and alternative walks stick to lower terrain.

Drive down the road, go under

Puente de Aguila

the A7 *autovía* and turn right at the roundabout onto the N340. Almost immediately pass on your right the **Puente de Aguila**: this four-tier aqueduct is a 19th-century replica of the great aqueduct in Segovia. Proceed along the fertile coast with orchards, some under cover as protection from the elements, before passing along the upper reaches of **Nerja** (2.5km ✝♠✕🚻⊕). Cross the Río Chillar (4.5km) and, at a roundabout, turn right for Frigiliana on the MA5105, soon leaving behind the bustle of the coastal strip. The Río Chillar is deep down on the right as the road climbs steadily towards the sierras, with the conical peak of Cielo distinctive in the distance.

You pass La Molineta, the little huddle of houses shown on page 90, and theBar La Molineta on the right (8.6km ✕). These are on the route of Alternative walk 11, a circuit which begins and ends in Frigiliana. Even at this short distance from the coast, mountains dominate the landscape. A right turn at a roundabout (9km) takes you into **Frigiliana★** (✝♠✕). At a height of 435m, this typically picturesque and brilliantly white-washed mountain village was the last in the area to be abandoned by the Moors. The road winds through the main street to the spot at the head of the valley where the tourists congregate around a few bars, restaurants and shops. Bear left here, past the bus stop; then, at the roundabout fork right on the MA5105 again (where the left fork goes back to Nerja).

You are now contouring round the valley on a road (not shown on some maps) lined with palm trees. But we call it the 'mimosa road', because in spring mimosas provide huge splashes of yellow all the way along. The surrounding slopes are neatly planted with fruit trees, as the road climbs gradually, winding high above Frigiliana and passing several bar/restaurants (✕) en route, all commanding awesome views over the countryside. Traversing a short ridge (15km) you can see down into the valleys on both sides, with the high peaks of the Almijara looking mystical in the morning haze. To the right, the Reserva Nacional de Sierra de Tejeda extends to Salares and beyond. Start descending (19km) and catch sight of the huge bulk of Maroma (2065m) at the far end of the Sierra de Tejeda. It is the highest peak in the area, and vestiges of snow linger into early spring. Wind down through fertile slopes to a dip (23.5km), then bear right up to a junction. Turn left at the roundabout and take the higher of two roads ('Todas direcciones'), soon lined with eucalyptus trees. Descend to the next junction (24.5km) and turn right (signposted to Cómpeta). The turning left leads to Torrox (✝♠✕), a town which claims to have the best climate in Europe.

The road skirts the hillsides, gradually gaining altitude. On the left, across the *barranco*, the slopes are dotted with villas, *cortijos* and water tanks, all startlingly whitewashed. You are now entering wine country, with neatly planted vineyards. Close to many of the *cortijos* you will also notice small rectangular plots laid out side by side on the sloping inclines; they look like large graves with triangular headstones. These are *paseros*. Every year, for a couple of weeks in August, grapes are laid out to dry here to produce the *Pasos Malagueños* — raisins from Malaga that you see in boxes in

Frigiliana

supermarkets. The grapes are turned frequently to ensure thorough drying and are covered overnight to protect them from early morning dew. For the rest of the year these *paseros* lie fallow.

A *mirador* (📷) at the Pavo Real restaurant (32.5km ✕📷) and another two a little over 1km further on offer extensive panoramic views of the surrounding sierras. Climb for a while and, as you approach Cómpeta, dominated by the tall chimney of its old sugar mill, *ignore* the first roads leading into the eastern part of the village. Continue round the opposite side of the valley and then take the road which is also signposted to Canillas de Albaida. **Cómpeta**★ (39km ✝🏔✕M) is worth a short visit, perhaps taking in the wine museum, but don't attempt to drive beyond its main car park; the streets are more suited to donkeys and carts than cars. From here continue round the slopes, still climbing gently, to the charming and well kept village of **Canillas de Albaida** (41.6km). Just a few metres past the village entry sign, fork right uphill on a little road signposted (on the wall on the right-hand side) to 'Santa Ana'. It takes you to the 17th-century church of Santa Ana (42km ✝), built on a site which originally held a 9th-century Moorish shrine. Though it looks a bit crumbly, Santa Ana is whitewashed and still in use. Walk 12 starts about 3km along the road signed to the 'Zona Recreativa Fábrica de la Luz' (*P*12). After looking at the attractive church, take a peep over the sheer drops to the valley behind it.

Leave Canillas the way you came and wind back around the slopes and through the lower part of Cómpeta. When you reach the junction with the A7206 where you turned off for Canillas

(45.5km), carry straight on for Algarrobo. Pass a petrol station (46.5km 🚉) and, as you round the valley, again catch sight of Maroma, looking quite benign and belying its 2065m of altitude. Turn sharp right towards Archez (49km) and, now on the descent, you will see several more villages and *paseros*. Cross the substantial bridge over the Río Algarrobo y Sayalonga (51.8km) and take the second turn-off right, signposted to Salares (MA4108).

The slopes are more barren now, but vines still survive among the olives. Maroma is now straight ahead of you, as the road runs down into **Salares** (58km 🛈), the sleepy and picturesque village shown below. Take a stroll through its steep streets and seek out the 13th/14th-century square minaret which is now incorporated into the church. Continue up the road and on towards Sedella, perched on the slopes of the Sierra de Tejeda, with Maroma as backdrop. Pass the turn into Sedella (60.6km 🛈🏔✕) and continue down the road, signposted to Canillas de Aceituno. The road runs beneath Sedella, passing its hostal/restaurant as you leave the village behind. After negotiating more twists and turns, not far beyond the 'Termino Municipal de Canillas' sign you

Salares, a typical pueblo blanco, *and its bridge; below:* Nerja

come to La Rahige, a delightful picnic/camping area laid out on the slopes amongst tall pines (66.8km ⛺P*CT3a*).

The main road bypasses the very narrow streets of **Canillas de Aceituno** (69km) with its colourful balconies and gardens. Look out for the huge Embalse de Viñuela in the valley below — 5km away as the crow flies. Follow the long and winding road downhill and, after passing a large water storage tank on the left (76.8km), turn right on the A7205 (77.4km). You are now travelling in a northwesterly direction and, after passing a cafe/bar (✕) on the left and crossing the Río Bermuza, **Viñuela** comes into sight over to the left (79.7km ⛰✕).

Notice the enormous U-shaped pass in the mountains ahead: it's the Boquete de Zafarraya, shown on pages 98-99. Walk 13 comes down through this pass and ends at the village of **Puente Don Manuel** (also known as Puente de Salia; 83km ⛰✕🅿), a major junction with several restaurants. Alternative walk 13 is circular and starts about 5km north of here. Turn left across the bridge and then left again at the junction with the A402, signposted to Vélez Málaga. Just 1.3km along (84.3km), go left once more towards Viñuela; then, almost immediately, turn very sharp right under a bridge. The road veers left and round towards an hotel, perched on a hill and commanding magnificent views across the Embalse de Viñuela to the all-encompassing mountains.

Drive past the hotel (85.7km), with a further view of the *embalse* as the road runs just above it. You pass an *área recreativa* on the right (86.7km; *P*CT3b) just before turning right on the A402 (87km) for Vélez Málaga. Keep following Vélez Málaga, eventually on the A356. This good road descends rapidly, leaving the mountains behind and levelling out as it approaches the coastal plain (95km). The town of **Vélez Málaga** (98.6km ✝⛰✕🅿), capital of the Axarquía, has seen the passage of many civilisations and has taken the best from each to create the architecturally impressive and cultural centre that exists today.

Keep to the A356 ring road round the western edge of town, then take the second exit at the roundabout, following signs for 'N340a Costa/Torre del Mar' and going under the *autovía*. Enter busy **Torre del Mar** (104km ✝⛰✕🅿⊕) and follow signs for Almería along the coast. The N340a is a sorry contrast to the quiet attractive roads through the mountains; a ribbon of development runs along both sides with scarcely a break. At least some of the old strategic watchtowers still survive; access to them was by rope or ladder to the top!

Carry on past **Torrox Costa** (116km ⛰✕🅿), a village which boasts Roman remains, and **Nerja** (124km ✝⛰✕🅿⊕), to reach the turn-off left back to your starting point at the Cueva de Nerja (128km).

Car tour 4: ANTEQUERA AND THE LAKES

Torremolinos • *Parque Natural Torcal de Antequera* • (Antequera) • El Chorro Nature Reserve • Carratraca • Torremolinos

176km/109mi; 4h-5h driving
On route: ⊼ at Aguas del Torcal, Valle de Abdalajis; Picnics (see *P* symbol and pages 9-13): 14, CT4; Walk 14

The towering rock sculptures of the Parque Natural Torcal de Antequera, created by the action of rain and wind on soft limestone, almost defy belief and are no less captivating than the grand and often ornate architecture of Antequera itself. But there are yet more treats in store — the Lakes District with its spectacular gorge patrolled by vultures and a delightful spa village perched high on a rock.

Start from the **Aquapark** on the outskirts of **Torremolinos**. Turn left (north) towards Málaga on the car park access road (Calle de Cúba, parallel with the N340). Turn left (0.4km) at the 'Stop' sign and pass the Palacio de Congresos. Then turn right onto the *autovía* (1.4km), following signs for Málaga. Ignore exits and skirt around Málaga on what is called the *ronda* (ring road), looking out to the beckoning sierras. Keep following A45/Córdoba/Granada/Sevilla on the MA20, joining the A7 for a short time. You go through an underpass into an area of low hills and follow signposting for Antequera, which directs you off the *ronda* (18km) and onto the A45. Pass a petrol station (20km ⛽) followed almost immediately by signs to a *pantano* (reservoir); a botanic garden is near the reservoir — a visit, perhaps, for another day.

The road runs alongside the Río Guadalmedina and crosses it frequently. This river was responsible for frequent catastrophic floods in Málaga up until the beginning of the 20th century. The hills bear only a sparse covering of trees, and old and new *cortijos* tucked into the slopes look isolated and exposed. The Parque Natural Montes de Málaga, a heavily wooded area, lies to the right. Take Exit 124 (37km ⛽) for Casabermeja and Colmenar.

At the roundabout on the outskirts of **Casabermeja** (where the Arab cemetery is worth a visit) follow clear signposting for Villanueva de la Concepción without going into the village, past a major interchange. Keep following signs for Villanueva de la Concepción: these delightful roads (MA436, MA3404 and finally A7075) through rolling fields and healthy orchards takes you up to **Villanueva** (53km), a village stretched out along the foot of the barren mass of the Torcal. Pass a *fuente* (57km) and turn left off the road (59.4km), to enter the **Paraje Natural Torcal de Antequera★**. Drive uphill past a *mirador* (📷) to the main car park and visitor centre (*i*; 63.2km). Park safely before trying to take in the astonishing sights that greet you. On the right, before the building, is the start of the 1.8km-long walking trail shown on page 13, the 'Ruta Verde' (*P*CT4). Take care to follow the *green* markers as they lead you between the huge natural rock sculptures, and be aware that vipers and scorpions inhabit some of the nooks and crannies.

When you leave this natural

Antequera, dominated by its Moorish castle

'museum' of rock, drive back to the A7075 and turn left for Antequera (67km). The road drops steeply, sometimes in hairpin bends, through an area known as the Boca de Asno (Donkey's Mouth) and passes alongside the attractive *área recreativa* Nacimiento del Río de la Villa (☐), set out along a pretty canalised river with shallow falls and inviting pools. Pass the motorable track to it at the KM49 marker (74.5km) and continue alongside the river past several well-sited restaurants (✵) to a junction (77km). Antequera★ (79km ♦♦▲✵⊕), dominated by its castle, lies 2km to the right and is a splendid town to visit if you have the time.

But the main tour turns left on the A343 for Valle de Abdalajís and Alora. The barren Torcal overlooks rows and rows of olive groves but, as you leave it behind and head towards the Lakes District, the slopes become slightly more fertile. Ignore turn-offs and approach **Valle de Abdalajís** (94km ♦♦▲✵☐☐), where there are some signed walking trails, details of which are available at the tourist office or online. At the Y-fork just before the village, go right (it may be signed to El Chorro or the Hoel/Restaurante La Garganta. This narrow road takes you along the upper part of the village; where you have a choice, fork right uphill *except* where an 'El Chorro' sign directs you to the left.

You leave the village behind, winding and bumping along a delightful narrow mountain road, with cliffs on the right and fantastic views to the left. Beyond several *cortijos,* turn right for **El Chorro** (100.2km). You pass a couple of bar/restaurants (✵). On the steep twisting descent you have views over the whole **El Chorro Nature Reserve★**. Don't miss the **Caminito del Rey★** (King's Walkway) bridging the narrow gap between the cliffs. Reach the first of many restaurants, Restaurante La Garganta (▲✵), an old flour mill close to the railway station (104.4km). This is a good place to stop, wander about and look for vultures.

Driving on, turn sharp left to cross the bridge and turn right along the side of the lake. Join the many cars that park in the laybys to marvel at the sheer cliffs, the railway line and the Caminito del Rey clinging precariously to the cliff face along the narrow gorge (photos on the cover and page 103).

As you snake through the **Parque Natural de Ardales** notice the strange rock formations. At a junction/roundabout (111km) your eventual homeward route is to the left, but first turn right for a view of the lakes and the opportunity for a stroll. Pass a campsite and a couple of entrances to the park, then turn right (113.2km) on a road signed to Restaurante El Mirador and park at the restaurant. From here Walk 14 offers several alternatives — try at least the Short walk for a panoramic view of the lakes from the *mirador* (P14).

Drive back to the El Chorro junction/roundabout and continue straight on towards Ardales. The Embalse el Conde de Guadalhorce lies on the right and soon the town of Ardales, dominated by the remains of its old castle, comes into view. Follow a sign for Málaga (121km) and then another as you bypass Ardales on the A357. At 125km turn left to Carratraca. Drive round the foot of the village and park close to the Bar/Restaurante Martillo, at a junction which announces the full name of this spa village — **Balneario de Carratraca** (126km). This village is a 'must', but don't be tempted to drive up into it. Walk up the hill, noticing the imposing building, a 19th-century palace which now houses the Tourist Office in its octagonal tower and the *ayuntamiento* in the main part. Then walk down Calle Trinidad Grund; pass the Hostal Principe and turn off to the right to the old *balneario* with its network of baths and pools.

Return to your car and continue along the road towards Alora. Pass the Restaurante El Trillo and after just a few metres turn right on an unsigned road which zigzags steeply down the hill. Cross a stream and follow signs to Málaga, through a tunnel and back onto the A357. The orange groves will catch your eye as you drive back towards the coast — always arranged in neat rows and looking lush at any time of year, they stretch out into the distance on both sides of the road.

At a junction (141.7km) continue straight on, signed to Cártama and Málaga. Cross the Río Grande (148.2km), wide but often dry (🚍 at 151.5km). Ignore turn-offs to Alhaurín El Grande and Cártama, then take Exit 57 for Churriana (158.2km; 🚍).

Take the first exit off the roundabout, heading south on the A7052. Enter **Churriana** and turn left at the roundabout (169km). Go straight over two roundabouts but, at the next, roundabout (171km), take the Torremolinos exit onto the N340/MA21. Almost immediately, follow signs for Benalmádena and Algeciras, to join the A7. Leave this *autovía* at Exit 998, signed to the Palacio de Congresos. Follow further signs to the Palacio and, just beyond it, turn right to the Aquapark (176km).

Car tour 5: SIERRA DE MIJAS
Benalmádena Costa • Mijas • Puerto de los Pescadores • Fuengirola • Benalmádena Costa

55km/34mi; 1h30min driving

On route: Picnic (see *P* symbol and pages 9-13): 15; Walks 15, 16

Despite being short and never far from the coast, this tour introduces you to an impressive mountain ridge, fertile river valleys and a typically picturesque Andalusian village. There are several opportunities for short strolls or longer walks which will better acquaint you with the countryside. The tour can be accessed from anywhere along the coast, picking it up at its 6km point on the autovía at Exit 223.

Start in **Benalmádena Costa** on the N340 at the Puerto Deportivo roundabout with the stylised sails. From here one road leads down to the Puerto Marina, but you head west along the N340 towards Fuengirola and Marbella. The road runs along the coast passing many hotels, most of them high-rise. Just beyond the rather tasteless, red-painted Castillo de Bil Bil, one of Benalmádena's tourist attractions, turn right at a roundabout on the A368 (1.7km) for Arroyo de la Miel and Pueblo Benalmádena. This palm-lined avenue heads towards the Sierra de Mijas, alongside the Arroyo de la Miel whose waters create a narrow fertile valley on the left. Keep to the A368 through **Pueblo Benalmádena** (3km ▲▲✕) and beyond. The road is not always well signposted as it heads through roundabouts and one-way turns, so keep whatever you are using as a satnav handy. You want to *stay on the A368* and go under the AP7/E15 motorway towards Mijas (🅿).

Beyond the motorway the A368 narrows considerably as you drive below the thickly wooded slopes of the Sierra de Mijas. Over to the left, beyond the scattered villas, the concentrated mass of white houses clinging to the slopes is the pretty village of Mijas. Wind round to it, passing a small, old aqueduct on the left (15.5km) and a succession of entrances to some grand villas.

At a roundabout, the tour turns up to the right, following signposting to Coín, but **Mijas**★ (17km ⛪▲▲✕🅿⊕📷**M**) is just to the left and you may wish to potter around before continuing. Walk 15 starts in the main square at Mijas and traverses the eponymous sierra — exploring several points of interest, both man-made and natural.

The road to Coín, lined with tall eucalyptus trees, runs above Mijas and passes (17.7km) the zigzag trail up to the Ermita del Calvario (shown overleaf) — our first objective on Walk 15 and a delightful picnic site with glorious views (⛪📷*P*15). It's worth parking at the *mirador* just a little further along the road and making the pilgrimage up to the *ermita* past the stations of the cross. Then, instead of returning down the same path, you could follow Short walk 15 back to the road just beyond your car. From the *mirador* there is a panoramic view over Mijas. Notice particularly the bullring and the amphitheatre which you may not have noticed just strolling through the village.

Continuing along this attractive road, you pass below a large water

36 Landscapes of Andalucía

reservoir on top of a hill. Tucked in just beneath it is the former municipal dog pound (20km). This is the **Puerto Colorado**, where the tough Walk 16 to Pico Mijas begins and ends, but you *could* join Walk 15 here as well: it comes down off the slopes opposite this point and heads back to Mijas. Rounding a bend (22km) the green and fertile Entrerrios valley comes into sight, with the peaks of the Sierra Blanca as the backdrop. This is the valley through which the Río Alaminos and the Río de Ojén flow before uniting to form the wide Río Fuengirola.

The Alhaurín Golf and Country Club (23.5km) is overlooked by a strange tower perched on top of a hill. It's interesting enough to warrant closer inspection, so drive on to the roundabout (25.7km) at **Puerto de los Pescadores** and take the second exit, signposted to Coín. A little way along on the right, park at the start of a chained access road and make your way up one of the steep paths which take you directly to the tower, the **Castillo de la Mota**. It was built in the late 1980s as a 'feature', when the surrounding area was earmarked for more golf-related development. But plans lapsed, and it now stands as an empty shell, covered with graffiti.

Car tour 5: Sierra de Mijas

Walk all round it, taking in the magnificent 360-degree views. To the west is the Sierra de las Nieves, dominated by Torrecilla (1919m) and, further round to the right, are the twin peaks of Prieta (1521m).

Go back to the roundabout and turn right, heading south towards Fuengirola on the A7503. Drive through orange groves and rolling grassy hills and notice the *alcornoques*, cork oak trees, on the left (30.6km). Over to the right, on the distant slopes, look carefully, and you may spot some Minas de Talco (talc mines). As you descend a little into a heavily wooded valley, the coast comes into sight. Citrus groves and lush vegetation grow along the valley of the Río Alaminos (34.8km) and, a little further on, is one of the valuable avocado plantations that the area supports.

Carrying on towards the coast (40km ⚐) and following the Río Fuengirola, the Sierra de Mijas becomes ever more prominent, and the Castillo de Sohayl stands sentinel on a mound on the outskirts of **Fuengirola** (🛏▲✕⚐⊕△). If you wish to sample the delights of this typical coastal resort, go straight ahead at a roundabout (41.4km). But to continue the tour, join the A7 *autovía* by following signposting towards Málaga.

Take Exit 211, signposted to Benalmádena Costa (43.6km) and rejoin the N340. Up on a hill, a *torre* and a *toro* compete for your attention, looking disdainfully down on unattractive tower blocks. Pass through several small resorts and, at a roundabout (51km), go straight on into Benalmádena Costa. Follow the road all the way past the Mijas turn-off you took on the outward journey and back to the Puerto Deportivo roundabout (55km).

Ermita del Calvario (Walk and Picnic 15). Encircled by the Sierra de Mijas, this picnic setting affords far-reaching views over the village of Mijas and agricultural land, all the way to the coast.

Car tour 6: SIERRA DE LAS NIEVES

Marbella • (Istán) • San Pedro • Ronda • El Burgo • Guaro • Monda • Ojén • Marbella

150km/93mi; about 4h driving; Detour to Istán: 25km/15.5mi; 45min
On route: ⌐ at Llanos del Plano, Quejigales; Picnics (see *P* symbol and pages 9-13): 17a-b, 18a-b, 19a-b, CT6; Walks 17-20

This tour takes you to Ronda, steeped in centuries of history, and to some of the other *pueblos blancos* (white villages) of Andalucía. But essentially it is a circuit of the Parque Natural Sierra de las Nieves. This vast expanse of outstanding natural beauty is crossed by high sierras and narrow deep gorges which support a great wealth of flora and fauna. From your car you will see fantastic scenery, but to do the area justice you should take advantage of the many opportunities to leave your car and explore inside the park. To make the most of the trip, choose a day which is forecast clear and sunny and set off early. (Remember, however, that it can be quite chilly at high altitude, even when the sun is shining.) If you wish, this tour can be picked up on the autovía at the 0.3km-point (the Plaza de Toros exit) or the 12km-point (the Ronda exit) and can be combined with Car tour 7, which is a circuit from Ronda.

Referring to the town plan on the reverse of the touring map, start at the roundabout on Duque de Lerma by the Plaza de Toros in **Marbella**: take the Ojén road (A355) towards the hills. Walk 17 starts a kilometre or so up this road and follows an old trail to the Olivar de Juanar, the olive groves of an old aristocratic hunting lodge, now a Hotel Parador. At just 0.3km, at the McDonald's roundabout, follow Algeciras signs onto the AP7/A7/E15 expressway *(autovía),* heading west. Attractively landscaped gardens attached to villas, restaurants, residential complexes and golf courses reach down to the roadside. So drive with care, watching out for vehicles seeking to enter the fast flow of traffic. Ignore signs for the motorway (AP7; the *autopista*); the A7 *autovía* passes through a tunnel

Car tour 6: Sierra de las Nieves

(5.7km), and shortly thereafter (7.3km) you have the opportunity to take the 25km detour described on page 42 — to Istán: take Exit 176, driving into the mountains, to the charming village of Istán (Walk 18).

The main tour continues along the A7/N340, crosses the Río Guadiza (11.6km) and, on the outskirts of **San Pedro**, turns right at traffic lights to take Exit 1053 (12km; signposted to Ronda). This winding road (several 🅿) heads towards the Sierra de las Nieves. It climbs steadily and, if you are behind a heavy vehicle, is slow going. Be patient — and grateful that you are not on the old road, crumbling sections of which can still be seen. You pass the well-known La Quinta golf course and then the village of La Heredia set behind graceful trees.

All the trappings of the coast are left behind as the road climbs steadily. Pine trees cling precariously to loose rocky slopes on either side and, in March, the large white flowers of the gum cistus plant attract attention. Soon (starting from about 25km) frequent viewpoints with good parking (📷) offer spectacular panoramas. As the composition of the rock changes abruptly, the reddish colour gives way to light grey, and the slopes become stark and barren (40km). A statue in contemporary style signals the highest point on the road at the **Mirador de Igualeja** (44km; 1125m 📷), at the start of a small plateau. Three kilometres further on a well-signed dirt road goes off right (47km) at the western

Ronda's church

40 Landscapes of Andalucía

entrance to the Quejigales area of the **Parque Natural Sierra de las Nieves★**. Walk 20, which climbs through the *pinsapo* forests shown on pages 6-7 and up to the Peñón de los Enamorados (1780m) starts about 10km along this dirt road (🅿) — but if you follow it for only 2km, you will reach a delightful picnic spot (*P*CT6) where you can enjoy a stroll.

The tour continues on the main road (✖ and ☕ at 49km); go straight on at all road junctions and you will begin to descend gradually. Your first glimpse of the white houses of Ronda comes at about 53km. The old part of the town, dominated by its church, lies to the left (west) of the town, close to the famous Tajo Gorge. Spectacular to look at, this gorge splits the town in two and is the resting place of many unfortunate souls — from the architect of the 18th-century bridge who fell to his death here as he tried to retrieve his hat to the hundreds of prisoners thrown into the depths by an angry mob during the Civil War.

The gradient steepens as you descend to cross a fertile plain, following signs to Sevilla at a roundabout (57km). Considering the altitude and the rugged nature of the encircling mountains, the gentleness of the landscape is an unexpected surprise. Cross the Río Guadalevín and reach a major roundabout on the eastern outskirts of **Ronda★** (61km ⛪🚌🚠✖☕⛽M). Car tour 7 starts at this roundabout and completes a circuit inside the Parque Natural de la Sierra de Grazalema — vulture country. This tour turns right, towards El Burgo on the A366, but first spend some time in Ronda, a fascinating town whose conquest by several different nations is reflected in its present architecture and culture.

From Ronda return to the roundabout and head towards El Burgo. The sometimes narrow and bumpy road runs parallel with the railway line, and both are spanned by a fine Roman aqueduct (63km) — incomplete, but impressive none the less. After crossing a plain planted with olive and oak trees, the road undulates across open hillsides, gradually climbing to **Puerto del Viento**, a pass at 1190m (72km 📷).

Descend from the pass enjoying that 'top-of-the-world' feeling always engendered when mountain peaks spread out beneath you. In stark contrast to the Ronda side of the pass, the surrounding slopes here are almost free from trees — including the desolate-looking Sierra de los Merinos ridge directly ahead, traversed by a line of pylons. But it all changes again soon after you negotiate a spectacular narrow defile between high cliffs and pass through the mountains. Wooded slopes overlook the valley of the Río del Burgo and, in autumn, the broad-leaved trees bordering the river create a pretty picture (see opposite).

The road descends sharply through pines to the **Mirador del Guarda Forestal** (81km 📷) where an elevated monument, 250m from the road, overlooks the route of Walk 19 deep down in the river valley. El Burgo soon comes into sight below, but it's still a long way down. After more twists and turns, a stand of tall eucalyptus trees welcomes you to **El Burgo** (86km 🚌✖☕), which overlooks a picturesque gorge filled with prickly pears. Drive straight

Picnic 19a: autumnal colours paint a vivid canvas at the first dam on the Río del Burgo.

through, following signs to Málaga and noticing the impressive Sierra de Prieta rising on the left. At the far end of the village, cross the bridge over the Río del Burgo. Just below the bridge is the starting point for Walk 19. You'll have to follow the entire walk to reach the beautiful setting shown on page 122, but its two short versions start here as well: Short walk 1 leads to the setting shown opposite (*P*19a), and Short walk 2 visits a charming shrine at the Fuensanta *zona recreativa* (♣⌒△*P*19b). A little further on, a track going off to the right (88km) also leads to Fuensanta, which is about 3km away.

The road zigzags out of the fertile plain, goes through the **Puerto de las Abejas** (820m) and descends through olive groves to **Yunquera** (94km 🅘 ▲ ✕ 🍺). The prominent old Arabic watchtower here, the Torre Vigía, is an information centre for the park. Following signs to Málaga, leave the village behind and pass through a stone arch (the Puente Palo), which used to carry an aqueduct. For as far as the eye can see, almost every inch of land has been cultivated. The sierras ahead, magnificent at any time, are at their best when silhouetted against the setting winter sun.

Once again, parts of the tortuous old road are a reminder of times past, when mules rather than vehicles passed this way. Even now, mules would perhaps be more appropriate for the steep road you pass (99km) going down to the tiny picturesque hamlet of Jorox, tucked into the hillside and surrounded by citrus orchards. Wind down past the Granja Escuela (Farm School) and at the **Alozaina** roundabout (104km ▲✕🍺) go right for Tolox, Málaga and Coín (still the A366). Eucalyptus trees again grow close to the road as you descend through the still intensely-cultivated countryside. Cross the Río Grande, its grassy banks lined with giant reeds and lush green vegetation, and pass the right turn to Tolox, the main eastern entrance to the natural park (109km ▲). Follow the Río Grande past villas and restaurants (✕) with colourful gardens and cross the Río Seco. Veer right, climbing away from the river, and take the right turn towards Guaro just before the 55KM road marker (118km).

Now on the A7100, you come into **Guaro** (123km ♣▲✕🍺), self-styled 'Paraíso de los Almendros' (Almond Paradise) — a name best appreciated at the beginning of the year when this whole valley is resplendent in pink and white blossom. Drive through, following signs to Marbella. Keeping to the A7100, you then pass above the rest of the village.

Monda soon appears ahead, dominated by a hill on which the meagre remains of its old castle are dwarfed by a modern luxury hotel. The road circles the hill and takes you through the outskirts of **Monda** (127km ✝■▲✖M). Pass the *lavadero* (wash-house) and *fuente* on the right and immediately turn sharp right for Ojén and Marbella *(not signposted when last checked)*. Pass a track on the right signposted to the Refugio de Juanar (129km) and ascend, again following Ojén and Marbella signposting, to join the A355.

You pass a place called Llanos de Pula (133km ⌐) and then a road to the Refugio de Juanar. Short walk 17 starts 5km up that road and goes to a *mirador* (*P*17b). Just beyond the Puerto de Ojén (580m), leave the main road: turn off left on the A7103 (134.5km) for a visit to Ojén. Descend into the green valley of the Río de Ojén, where thick vegetation conceals any sign of its old iron, copper, nickel and lead mines. The coast comes into sight before you enter **Ojén★** (138km ▲✖☕), a typical Andalusian white village in which the friendly locals maintain old customs and traditions. Drive above the main part of the village, to the petrol station at the far end. Alternative walk 17, a delightful hillside ramble, starts and ends here.

Continue up to the main road, following signs for Marbella. As you drive back to the coast, admire the views and continue down to your starting point at the Plaza de Toros roundabout (150km).

Detour to Istán

From the 7.3km-point of the tour take Exit 1048 towards Istán/A7176. At the roundabout, take the first exit (signposted to Istán). The road runs high above the exceptionally lush valley of the aptly named Río Verde, Green River, and passing under the AP7 motorway. In places the narrow and winding old road can be seen on the right.

Pause at the *mirador* (6km 📷) for a view of the Embalse de la Concepción, which collects the water that drains from some of the highest points in the park. Pass an *ermita* and the driveway to a hotel/restaurant which commands unrivalled views over Istán and the valley of the Río Verde, then come into **Istán★** (14.5km ✝▲✖), set high above the northern tip of the *embalse*. At the entrance to the village, fork right uphill, to the parking area (being a typical *pueblo blanco*, its streets are narrow, so explore on foot). Walk 18, which starts from the car park, provides a feast for the eyes in the southern part of the park. If you don't have time for that, at least try the short walk which takes you a little way out of the village (*P*18a; photo on page 118) before returning for a stroll along some of its attractive streets (photo on page 116) and well-sited *miradores* (*P*18b).

Car tour 7: SIERRA DE GRAZALEMA

Ronda • Villaluenga del Rosario • Benaocaz • Ubrique • El Bosque • Benamahoma • Puerto del Boyar • Grazalema • Ronda

122km/76mi; 3h30min-4h driving
On route: 🅿 at Las Covezuelas, Los Cañitos, Los Llanos del Campo; Picnics (see *P* symbol and pages 9-13): 21-23; Walks 21-23

Actually a massif comprising about 16 different sierras, the Sierra de Grazalema has its own microclimate which occasions the highest rainfall in Spain. Botanically speaking it is a wonderland of variety and colour, while its mountains, valleys and rivers provide magnificent walking country. Vultures breed here, and the whole area to the north of the road joining Benamahoma to Grazalema is protected. You must have authorisation to walk there, and from January to June (the nesting season), you must walk accompanied by a guide. This tour, which can be linked with Car tour 6, is a clockwise circuit inside the Parque Natural de la Sierra de Grazalema. Whether you are climbing through high passes or driving through charming *pueblos blancos* (white villages), look for the vultures soaring and circling above. Those in a large group are likely to be griffon vultures, while solitary birds may be black vultures. With a wingspan of almost three metres (nine feet), they present quite a sight!

Start from the main roundabout on the eastern outskirts of **Ronda**, following Sevilla signs on the A374, the Ronda bypass. Cross a steeply-inclined railway line, wind down into a fertile agricultural plain and cross the Río Guadalcobacín (7.5km). Pass the turn off for Setenil, a village whose streets are set into the rocks. Its name is said to derive from the words meaning 'seven nil', in recognition of the fact that the Christians failed seven times to

Embalse de Zahara

take it from the Moors. Climb gently out of the plain between wooded slopes, ignoring the turn to Montejaque (15km) and taking the next turn-off (16.3km), the A372 signposted to Grazalema. At 17.7km you leave the A372 (your return route from Grazalema), continuing straight ahead through a pass, the **Puerto de Montejaque** (A2300).

With the Sierra Margarita ahead to the left, drive down between cultivated fields to the Embalse de Zahara, overlooked by the remains of Zahara castle. From now on keep your eyes open for vultures, but don't forget to pay attention to your driving as well.

Just before the bridge near the southern tip of the reservoir, turn left (25km) on the CA9123, signposted to Grazalema). This narrow road carries few vehicles and, in the summer, you will often see little owls perched on the posts along the verge, behaving for all the world as if they were traffic wardens. Surrounded by craggy hills and wooded slopes, the road winds through an amazingly beautiful valley, where a few *cortijos* rely mainly on olives to provide a meagre living. Whatever the time of year, there will always be colour, whether the reds and golds of the autumn trees, the white of the snow-capped peaks, or the delightful and varied hues of wildflowers and shrubs.

Beyond the Ermita de Nuestra Señora del Rosario (31km ✝), as the gradient increases, a few hairpin bends take you up through an area of holm oaks to a crest from where Grazalema can be seen tucked into the slopes ahead (photo on pages 128-129). You will pass through the village later so, at the T-junction (34km), turn left on the A372, following signs for Ronda and Ubrique. Wind downhill and cross the Río Guadalete, with the impressive Sierra del Caillo across the valley to the left. Pass a left turn to Ronda (your return route, the A372) and start descending, with rocky hills and steep cliffs to the right and open meadows where cattle graze to the left. In summer woodchat shrike perch on overhead cables.

Now on the A374, you pass Las Covezuelas, a shady haven with a *fuente* (44km ⚲△), before emerging from the woods to gorse-covered slopes and a cultivated valley which leads to **Villaluenga del Rosario** (46.5km), the highest village in the province of Cádiz. With cliffs to either side, drive down the aptly named Manga (Sleeve) de Villaluenga, a spectacularly narrow valley. Look out for blue rock thrushes that are attracted by the drystone wall that snakes all the way through this valley and stop to admire the views from the attractive **Mirador del Cintillo Aguas Nuevas** (50km 📷), with information panel, benches, a panoramic photograph naming all the surrounding sierras and a bird-identification panel.

Wind down below the *mirador* and, immediately after a *fuente*, turn right on a little slip road to **Benaocaz** (52km ✝▲✕), an ancient settlement created by the Moors in the 7th century and still retaining many old traditions. (Park and walk through the village if you like, then continue the tour along the main road.) Walk 22, a glorious trek through the mountains (photo on page 135), starts from the village and offers a a couple of shorter options, one of

Grazalema: once a focus of the wool trade, the village now has a reputation for handicrafts and culinary delights.

which leads to the river (*P*22). Drive along the narrow streets, some with crazy paving, and when you are faced with a No Entry sign ahead, turn down very steeply to the left. Turn left at the junction by the church, back onto the main road.

As you pass a leather factory and a junction (58km), **Ubrique** (✝︎▲✕🅿︎⊕), a substantial but not particularly noteworthy town, is just off to the left. The tour turns right on the A373, following signposting for Villamartín. Within about 1km you will begin to see, through a gap over to the right, the Salto del Cabrero (Goatherd's Leap), a gigantic cleft caused by a geological fault. This is one of the highlights on Walk 22 and one of its short versions. Don't forget to keep looking out for vultures as you descend sharply to cross the Río Tavizna, where there is an old bridge on the left (65km).

Turn right on the A372 at a junction for Grazalema and Benamahoma (67km). Some of the place names around here are relics of the Arabic past, with the prefix 'Ben' having the same connotation as the Scottish 'Mac'. At 69km another park recreation zone, Los Cañitos (🅰︎), lies just on the outskirts of **El Bosque** (▲✕△), a cool and beautiful village with a trout hatchery, botanical garden and visitor centre. Walk 23 comes here from Benamahoma by way of the delightful riverside path shown overleaf. The tour runs along the edge of the village and turns right (70km), following signposting for Benamahoma. The road is pleasantly shaded with a variety of trees, including eucalyptus, and the Sierra del Pinar, where the *pinsapo* still survives, rises spectacularly ahead. You pass the left turn to the lower section of **Benamahoma** (75km ✕△), which also boasts a trout hatchery and where Walk 23 begins (*P*23). Wind up steeply round some hairpin bends, taking in the views back down over the Benamahoma valley.

Beyond the *área recreativa* Los Llanos del Campo (78km 🅰︎△), continue climbing past some laybys (📷) — one with an information board detailing a short walk to Cerro de la Mesa (Table

Río Majaceite, not far beyond the setting for Picnic 23

Mountain); this path is, however, sometimes closed because of fire risk. Not far past the km42 road marker, there is a small viewpoint with a *fuente*, from where you can see the Salto del Cabrero again. Can you spot any of the vultures that regularly patrol the cliffs on the left? Beyond the **Puerto del Boyar** (1103m; 85km) you come to a stone picnic shelter (*merendero*; **P**21) a little further down the road. With the Río Guadalete rising close by, it's a good spot to pause and have a stroll. Walk 21 (photo on page 130) heads into the mountains from here, while Walk 22 comes up from Benaocaz and returns via the Salto del Cabrero.

Continuing the tour, begin a steep descent below craggy rock formations overlooking thickly wooded slopes. On coming to a junction (87km) ignore the left fork to Zahara and Algodonales, two villages at the top end of the reservoir; keep ahead towards Grazalema (still on the A372). Cross the Río Guadalete once more; Walk 21 leaves the road here on its way to the *merendero*. As it descends from the Llano de las Presillas, Walk 21 crosses our route — at Camping Tajo Rodillo (88km △). Follow signposting straight on to the centre of **Grazalema**★ (89km ✝♦✕₽). The road runs above the village then winds down through the main street, where you can park. Then continue past the petrol station on the outskirts of the village. At the junction with your outward route (91km), carry straight on to the Puerto de Los Alamillos (822m; 94km), where you turn left for Ronda (still the A372).

The surrounding slopes are again heavily wooded, mainly with cork oaks, and you may pass strips of bark sitting in piles at a small cork factory on the right (103km). Leaving the woods behind, keep following signs for Ronda, going right at a junction (104.5km) and then right again on the A374 (106km). This road takes you back to the roundabout where you started (122km).

Walking

Spain is the second most mountainous country of Europe, with some ranges extending almost to the coast. Many visitors content themselves with admiring the mountains from their loungers by the hotel pool, but that is no substitute for being out there among them. The car tours take you closer, but it is only on the walks that you can enjoy the complete countryside experience. Andalucía is particularly well endowed with nature's blessings and you will delight in the beauty and variety of its flora and fauna. At almost any time of year flowers and trees provide a kaleidoscope of colour. The Nature notes on pages 6-7 explain a little about the interesting things you will encounter most frequently on the walks. *There is something here for everyone*, with the short walks well within the capabilities of most people, even if the main walks are too long or strenuous.

A few of the walks are linear or 'out-and-back', but the majority are circular, this being not only more practical but also more satisfying. In order to complete circuits, we have sometimes had to include stretches on asphalt roads. But these are always quiet country roads, and you are unlikely to meet any traffic on them. However, do remember that roads and tracks leading to official picnic sites will be crowded and noisy on Sundays and *fiesta*s, when the local people like to have a day out.

It would be unusual while walking if you did not see another soul all day. Even in the more remote areas you will come across goatherds, as well as farmers tending their groves and terraces. Strolling the highways and byways is also a favourite pastime among the villagers themselves. All the people you meet will appreciate a greeting, so say *Hola* (Hello), *Buenos días* (Good morning) or *Buenas tardes* (Good afternoon) when you meet the local people.

It is important that all walkers read and *heed* the country code on pages 7-8.

Grading, waymarking, maps, GPS

We've tried to give you a quick overview of each walk's **grade** in the Contents. But many of our walks have shorter or alternative versions. In the Contents we've only had space to show the *lowest* grade of a *main* walk: for full details, see the walk itself: there is plenty of variety in almost every walk.

Here is a brief overview of the three gradings:
- easy — suitable for anyone who is reasonably fit and active
- moderate — requires stamina; may involve some fairly easy scrambling
- strenuous — will appeal to experienced sure-footed hill walkers

Any of the above grades may be followed by:
- particularly challenging exposure; danger of vertigo

Grading walks is a tricky business. People who can walk all day on the flat without tiring may find even short uphill sections very strenuous. Others who experience no problems on prolonged climbs might nevertheless feel that a three-hour walk is quite long enough. At the start of each walk description we have tried to give a good indication of what to expect, but *if you read the entire walk description* before setting off, you will have an even better picture. Some walks are very long, and others involve steep inclines, going through tunnels, wading in rivers or scrambling on rocky mountain slopes. Be sure to choose walks that are within your capability, remembering that *enjoyment* is the primary aim.

Navigation in the mountains of Andalucía is relatively straightforward, and on the one or two occasions where confusion could occur we have made the walk instructions as clear and comprehensive as possible. A few of the walks follow sections of well-established routes and you will come across a variety of **waymarks**. There are the red- and white-striped markings of the GR (*Gran Recorrido*) long distance footpaths, the yellow and white of the PR (*Pequeño Recorrido*) short distance walks, and the green and white stripes of *Senderos Locales* (local walks, usually under 10km). Elsewhere there may be coloured dots or arrows, marker posts, or cairns — or a combination of all of these. However, *our walks do not rely on waymarks and, indeed, some can be quite deceptive. It is wise to **follow our written instructions** at all times.*

The **maps** in this book are based on Openstreetmap mapping (see page 2), but have been very heavily annotated from our notes and GPS work in the field. We hope that these maps, which we have found to be *very* accurate on the ground, will be a boon to walkers. It is a pity that we have to reproduce them at only 1:50,000 to keep the book to a manageable size; quite a few walkers buy both the paperback *and* download our pdf files so that they can enlarge the maps — or you can enlarge them on a colour photocopier.

Free **GPS track** downloads are available for all our walks: see the Andalucía page on the Sunflower website. Please bear in mind, however, that GPS readings should *never* be relied upon as your sole reference point, as conditions can change overnight. *But even if you don't use GPS*, it's great fun opening our GPX files in Google Earth to preview the walks in advance!

Where to stay

Our walks are spread over a huge area, so wherever you are based, *some* of them will be easily accessible. Most visitors stay on the coast but, if your main interest is *walking*, it is a good idea to find accommodation in the mountains. That way you can tackle several walks in an area without too much driving. You can now find good hotels, apartments and *pensiones* in smaller towns and villages; many can be booked via the Internet. Capileira, Cumbres Verdes in the Sierra Nevada, Cómpeta, Viñuela, Colmenar, El Burgo, Grazalema and Benaocaz are just a few of the places which would be suitable centres.

Getting about

The coastal strip and main routes inland are quite well served with **buses**, but elsewhere timetables are designed to suit the local population rather than walkers. But it *is* possible to make use of buses for some of our walks and we have included the relevant timetables and web sites (see pages 141-142). They may vary according to season, so always check times before setting off. It is also worthwhile remembering that buses have a habit of passing intermediate places on their route much earlier than expected. In the villages, the bars or *tabacaleras* in the main square can usually tell you when buses run through, but do take their advice with a pinch of salt unless you see a written timetable. Note that not all tourist offices hold information about buses.

For some of the walks you could make use of a **taxi**, agreeing the fare in advance, or arrange to stay overnight close to the area where the walk starts.

But, undoubtedly, the best way of getting to the walks described in this book is by **car**. Hire one through your travel agent when arranging your holiday or book direct with a hire company. Prices are very reasonable in spring and autumn, which of course are the best seasons for walking. You *can* hire locally, but it is often more expensive and less easy to solve problems, should any arise.

Weather

The mountains of southern Spain protect the coast from the worst weather and contribute to the climate which

50   Landscapes of Andalucía

makes it so popular as a holiday destination. Undoubtedly the best seasons for walking are spring and autumn, when temperatures are comfortable and the countryside is at its colourful best. Whenever it is hot, attempt only the shorter walks, or those graded 'easy' — but, even then, be cautious in the sunshine. And avoid high level walks in winter, when the ground can be snow-covered for several months.

Walk 1: descending the old trail (Carihuelas)

Because this book covers such a large area, it is impossible to generalise about the weather; indeed, with the large variation in altitude on some of the walks, you might experience all four seasons in one day. Fierce storms can occur unexpectedly at almost any time of year, so make sure you are prepared. Temperatures in the mountains can be extreme, falling as low as −15°C and rising to over 40°C — with wind and wildfires.

In the Sierra Nevada and the Alpujarra, the main rains tend to come in autumn. The Sierra de las Nieves and the Sierra de Grazalema are wettest from December to February, the latter range having the highest recorded rainfall in Spain. Much of the rain is torrential and falls in short periods of time, so there are usually plenty of dry sunny days. Of course the rain falls as snow in the mountains.

Always take account of prevailing conditions: a warm sunny day can turn bitterly cold with the passage of just a few clouds. Other than using your smartphone, obtain local forecasts if possible. We have found these to be quite reliable.

What to take

The time of year and prevailing weather conditions will largely dictate what you should carry with you. But things can change rapidly in the mountains and with even the lowest sierras rising to over 1000m, it is best to equip yourself for all eventualities on all the walks.

For sun protection, take **suncream, sunhat** and **long-sleeved shirt**. For the mountains, take **warm** and **waterproof clothing**. The whole area tends to be very rocky underfoot, so wear **stout, thick-soled shoes, preferably with ankle support** (for comfort we recommend proper lightweight hiking boots). Telescopic **trekking poles** are very useful, as there are many steep, rough descents. Be prepared for paths and tracks to be muddy for a day or so after heavy rain. The other essential is **water**. There are *fuentes* on many of the walks, but in summer you may find they are dry (and in the Alpujarra the water often tastes bitter). For all longer walks you should take a **picnic** and some high-energy food. All the walks can be followed without a **compass**, but it would be foolish to tackle any of the high mountain ones without one or a GPS. *Do* carry a **mobile/smartphone** (the **emergency number is 112**), **first-aid kit**, extra water, a couple of large black bags, whistle, torch and extra warm clothing. Where necessary, we specify extra items.

52   Landscapes of Andalucía

Potential hazards

Dogs should present little threat. The fiercer ones are chained up or fenced in, while those left to run loose, though noisy, lively and curious, are harmless. But *do* carry a 'Dog Dazer' if dogs worry you; these are widely available on the web. We have seen neither **snakes** nor **scorpions** on our walks, but they *do* exist — so be careful when walking through scrub, and don't disturb rocks and stones. A huge variety of **mushrooms** appear in damp areas, particularly in autumn. Some are likely to be highly poisonous, so don't be tempted to pick, or even touch, any of them. **Deep gorges** should also be treated with care and caution.

Organisation of the walks

The walks chosen for this book represent the best walking areas within a vast region. We have divided them into seven groups, stretching from the Almuñécar area (Sierra Nevada and Alpujarra), through Nerja/Torre del Mar (Sierra de Almijara), the Lakes District, Torremolinos/Fuengirola (Sierra de Mijas) to Marbella (Sierra de las Nieves and Grazalema). *Wherever you are staying, there will be easily accessible one-day walks.*

Begin by taking a look at the fold-out touring map and locating those nearest to you. The route notes and detailed map will give you an idea of what to expect. Every itinerary begins with planning information — distance, grade, how to get there, what to take, and the total ascent/descent. This should tell you whether the walk is within your capabilities. Wherever possible, we suggest shorter and alternative walks.

Our **timings** do not include any lengthy stops for birdwatching, picnicking, or the like. Allow for these, and also the weather: hot sun, driving rain, and strong winds will affect your progress. Check the walking notes frequently to avoid missing turn-offs or landmarks. After a couple walks, you should be able to adjust our timings to your own pace.

The following symbols are used on the walking maps:

Symbol	Meaning	Symbol	Meaning	Symbol	Meaning
	main road	540	height (metres)	●	snow pit *(nevera)*
	secondary road	🚐	bus stop	♪	spring, tank, etc
	motorable track	🚗	car parking	∩ ■	cave.building
	other track	📷	best views	△	rock formation
-----	footpath	✝	church.chapel	⌐	information panel
	river, stream, *acequia*	†	shrine.cross	⛯	hydroelectric plant
3→	main walk	■△	castle.camping	⎍ ∩	factory.aqueduct
3→	variation	✸✗	mill.quarry	❀ ⎲	garden.monument
3→	other described walk	🎋	picnic tables	P	picnic (see page 9)

Walk 1: BUSQUÍSTAR • BAÑOS DE PANJUILA • FERREIROLA • ATALBEITAR • BUSQUÍSTAR

See also photograph page 50
Distance: 9.5km/5.9mi; 3h43min
Grade: ●-●: moderate-strenuous, with ascents/descents of about 450m/1475ft overall — a few of them steep, but none prolonged. You must be sure-footed and have a head for heights. Many way-markings in this area (PR, GR, wooden posts, painted boards).
Note: a small stretch of the main walk path, just after the 2h07min-point, is prone to landslips. It is now in good repair but, if the problem recurs, you will have to follow Alternative walk 1 back to Busquístar.
Equipment: see page 51; *walking boots are essential.*
How to get there and return: 🚗 or 🚌 to/from Busquístar (the 81km-point on Car tour 1); park in car park near the church square (36° 56.252'N, 3° 17.627'W), where the bus also stops. 🚌 from Granada takes 2h55min! Not in the time-tables, bus departs Granada bus station daily at 10.00 and 12.00, returns at 16.13 and 17.28. *Recheck these times at www.alsa.es!*
Short walk: Río Trevélez (2km/1.2mi; 44min). ● Easy, with descent and corresponding ascent of just 150m/500ft; equipment as on page 51; access as main walk. Follow the main walk to the 20min-point by the river and the mill and return the same way.
Alternative walks
1 Baños de Panjuila (8.5km/5.3mi; 2h43min). ● Moderate, with ascents and corresponding descents of 420m/1380ft, some of them steep; equipment and access as main walk. Follow the main walk to **ⓐ**, then take the signposted GR142 up to the right and, with Busquístar visible ahead and fantastic views of the valley below, climb gradually, passing a huge precarious-looking overhang. The path descends from here to cross a MOTORABLE TRACK (2h23min), continuing through trees and above terraces, undulating gently towards the village. An earthen path takes you across a bridge, and you begin the steep climb to the FIRST OF THE HOUSES (2h40min), where walls and balconies are festooned with flowers or, in autumn, *pimientos* (photo on page 1). Wind up through the village to the CHURCH SQUARE in Busquístar (2h43min).
2 Alpujarran villages (5.6km/3.4mi; 2h14min). ● Moderate, with ascents/descents of 250m/820ft. Follow the main walk to the 6min-point at the 'CAMINO AL RÍO' SIGN and carry on straight ahead until, in just a few minutes, you see a walk signpost to 'CAMINO A FERREIROLA'. Follow this path (Alternative walk 1 in reverse) to **ⓐ** (43min). Turn right, picking up the main walk at the 2h-point following it to the end at Busquístar (2h29min).

This is probably as enjoyable and satisfying a walk as any we have ever done. With a starting point at 1160m, you are already in the heart of the mountains, and the high peaks will often be covered in snow. The landscape varies from gentle to rugged as you traverse the ancient paths and trails. Life in the little villages and *cortijos* along the route seems hardly to have changed in hundreds of years, and the mode of transport is still the horse or donkey. Although a fantastic walk at any time, it is particularly enjoyable in spring, when the wildflowers are at their colourful best, and snow still lingers on the mountain tops.

Start out from the leafy CHURCH SQUARE in **Busquístar** (**❶**) with its *fuente*, bar and bus stop. From the *mirador* overlooking the lower terraces, glance across to the hills on the far side of the valley, where some of the paths you will follow are visible. Then wind down the pretty concrete path at the side of the Bar Vargas, overlooking some typical Andalusian flat roofs.

As you leave the village behind, turn left with the GR142 (among others) at the 'CAMINO AL RÍO' sign (**6min**). *(Alternative walk 2 carries straight on here.)* A steep earthen path takes you between tall deciduous trees and terracing, passing above a BUILDING (**10min**) which has replaced an old *cortijo*. It levels out a little above cultivated plots, then steepens again and zigzags downhill, leaving the terracing behind. The distant sound of the water in the **Río Trevélez** filters up from below as the path becomes rocky and, by the time you reach the river, at a ruined GRAIN MILL and a BRIDGE (**❶**; **20min**; *P*1a), the noise can be quite thunderous.

Cross the bridge, then zigzag steeply up the trail on the far side. Pause and look back at the dam, at Busquístar and at the evergreen oaks that cling precariously to the hillside. The trail is substantial, and one feels quite secure despite the sheer drops into the valley. It is still used regularly by locals with their donkeys, and mint, sage and thyme grow in profusion all the way up.

At **42min** reach the brow and then skirt almost level around the hillside. Opencast iron mines can be seen across the *barranco* on the left and, in spring, the slopes are resplendent with broom and lavender. A gradual climb brings you to the once-bustling **Venta del Relleno** at a ROAD JUNCTION on the route of Car tour 1 (**❷**; **51min**). These old abandoned buildings are probably associated with the mines. Here you turn right (signposted to Torvizcón) and walk up this quiet road for a short distance towards the Cortijos de Panjuila. Notice the old **Acequia Real de Trevélez** over on the left. In the valley, beyond the groves of almonds, olives and figs, are the ruins of an old mercury mine. Listen for stonechats, warblers and rock sparrows which enjoy the solitude here and delight in flowering almond blossom.

Fork right to the **Cortijos de Panjuila** (**❸**; **1h13min**) and go up the track past the little white cottages, no longer permanently inhabited. Look out for the ravens which often soar above the hill ahead. Leave the main track which continues round the base of the hill, and take the initially-grassy PR-marked cart track going downhill past NO 4, THE LAST COTTAGE on the right. Enjoy the

This pretty fuente *near Ferreirola is called 'Fuente Gaseosa' in Spanish. Below: Busquístar*

company of the lively small birds and be prepared to flush some noisy partridge. At **1h26min** you reach the mineral spring and ruins of **Baños de Panjuila** (④; *P*1b). On the left, a little way past the ruins, is a tiny stone bridge which takes you to a *fuente*. Beyond the bridge some rocks above the old bathing pools provide a superb place to pause. On the slopes on the opposite side of the valley are perched eight little Andalusian villages, startlingly-white against the hillside. You will visit three of them before returning to Busquístar.

As the route, a bit overgrown and muddy at the outset, continues beyond the *baños*, stop and look across the valley. You will be able to see the route of the Alternative walk snaking directly up the rocky slopes in short zigzags.

But for now, continue on to the

medieval trail shown on page 50, the **Carihuelas** (**5**) — an amazing feat of engineering, with the steep slopes carefully stepped to ease the gradient. As the trail zigzags steeply down towards the river, you'll see the pipes and buildings of a disused hydroelectric plant (*fábrica de la luz*) and another old mill which still contains a few relics of its working past. Cross the BRIDGE over the river (**1h55min**) and continue on the PR-marked trail, bearing left past the MILL. Notice the old terraces across the river, where grain was grown for processing in the mills. The rocks are alive with wheatears and, in spring, you will be entertained by the musical song of serins.

As you pass along the top of terracing, you have your first views of Ferreirola and Pitres ahead. All the villages around here are connected by an amazing network of paths, and this walk samples only a few of them. Continue climbing gradually and take note of the waymarked GR142 up to the right (**a**; **2h**): *Alternative walk 1 follows this path; Alternative walk 2 comes down it.* When the trail opens out a little, cross an open expanse of rock, bear right into deciduous woods, then cross a stream (**2h07min**). Just beyond here is an area prone to landslips. (Should there have been a recent landslip and the way ahead looks unsafe, return to **a** and follow Alternative walk 1 back to Busquístar.)

Continue past a fine example of an *era* (threshing floor) on the left; it looks just like a balcony, with views over a little house and a *barranco* (**2h22min**).

When you reach the *fuente* shown on page 55, be warned that the water has a high mineral content — tasting a bit like soda water. Proceed up the slope and through **Ferreirola** (**6**; **2h33min**). During the time of the Arabs, this tiny village became one of the most important places in the Alpujarra because of its silk production and its four springs.

Just before the *lavadero* and the *fuente* at the entrance to the church square, turn right up a steep little road. The road becomes a lovely flower-lined trail (**Camino Medieval**) which takes you up to the foot of **Atalbéitar** village. When you meet the road (**7**; **2h52min**) turn right and walk through the village, always heading in the same direction. Pass a *fuente* with three spouts and join the GR7-waymarked path signed to PÓRTUGOS. At a signposted junction (**8**; **2h58min**) the path to the left goes up to Pórtugos. You continue straight ahead and are immediately faced with a brilliant view back down to Ferreirola. This charming path undulates around the slopes past another *era* (**3h04min**) and, as water thunders down a *barranco*, you round it to pass the ruins of a mill set high above the ravine.

Go left at a fork and climb steeply for a while, passing beside a little *cortijo* and above a more substantial one (**3h09min**). Ignore a path to the right (**3h16min**) and continue straight up, emerging into the open at the top of the steep rise. Skirt round the edge of some fields and meet a track coming from the left (**3h22min**). Follow it, noticing the sparklingly white houses of Busquístar ahead. At a junction, fork left, up to the main road (**3h25min**). Turn right and, back in **Busquístar** (**3h36min**), head down to the CHURCH SQUARE and your car (**3h43min**).

Walk 2: CAPILEIRA: THE THREE BRIDGES

Distance: 6km/3.7mi; 2h35min
Grade: ● strenuous, with ascents/descents of 540m/1770ft overall, including quite a steep climb at the end
Equipment: see page 51; trekking pole(s) useful
How to get there and return: 🚗 or 🚐 to/from Capileira (the 67km-point on Car tour 1); park near the bus stop and *ayuntamiento* in the centre of the village (36° 57.661'N, 3° 21.512'W).
🚐 from Granada takes about 2h. Not in the timetables, bus departs Granada bus station daily at 10.00 and 12.00, returns at 16.50. *Recheck these times at www.alsa.es!*

At an altitude of around 1435m/4700ft, Capileira is a fine starting point for walks into the Alpujarra. This delightful walk up the Poqueira Valley, mostly on old trails, takes in the three bridges which lie below Capileira. Draining from the high peaks of the Sierra Nevada, the river is always clear and fast-flowing, and the abundance of water makes it possible to exploit to the full the fertility of the surrounding countryside, much of it steeply sloping. Market gardens and cultivated terraces produce a variety of crops and fruit trees. In spring, herbs and delicate wildflowers line the paths, while in autumn, the huge spreading chestnut trees provide the splendour and the shade, and the crunch of nuts underfoot.

Puente Abuchite and the Río Poqueira

Capileira and the Veleta ridge

Start out at the *ayuntamiento* (town hall) **Capileira** (⭕): fork left off the main road, along the street called Dr Castilla. Walk to the end of this street and turn left into a little square (Plaza Calvario). Cross the square diagonally and, as you head out the other side, you'll see the Vista Veleta apartments ahead.

Walk to the right of the apartments, then turn sharp left downhill, noticing the village *mirador* off to the right. The road becomes a sealed track at the edge of the village, heading downhill past houses with animal pens on the ground floors. At the foot of the village, take the route going steeply downhill to the right, following signs MOLINO DE BUBIÓN and CAMINO DE LAS HIGUERILLAS ('FIG TREE WAY'; ❶). It turns sharp left below the village.

Keep heading down; in places the path is concreted. You pass fenced cultivation, where horse and plough are still regularly used, and come to a WATERCOURSE (**28min**) which always seems to be overflowing. Don't cross, but follow the watercourse briefly as the trail levels out and and turns to the right by a *cortijo*. Wind left past the *cortijo* and zigzag past some ruins, to a wide path (**39min**). Turn right and reach the valley floor near the first of the bridges, indicated by a hand-made sign, the **Puente del Molino** (❷; **46min**).

Cross the bridge and climb straight up the far side, to a T-junction. Looking up, you can just make out the lowest houses of Capileira on the opposite slopes. Turn right (PR-A401/PR-A70) and climb to the right of a *cortijo* — perhaps with yappy dogs (**57min**). Almost immediately after passing an abandoned hut and **threshing floor**, bear right on a pleasantly shady path which contours along the slopes, heading upriver.

Cross a stream and *ignore* a waymarking post directing you up to the left. Instead, go right, across another stream, and almost immediately reach a FORK (**1h18min**). Both routes lead to the same place, so take your pick and soon pass another WAYMARKING POST (**1h23min**). The path becomes overgrown in parts as it contours above a partly-ruined *cortijo*. Again faced with a choice of paths, take either of them and pass below a *cortijo*, to meet another path at a T-JUNCTION (**1h36min**). Turn right and descend to the river at the second bridge, the **Puente Chiscar** (also called 'Puente Chiscal' or 'Puente Chistal'; ❸; **1h42min**).

Cross this bridge and head uphill on a path which crosses a small *barranco* (**1h46min**).

Continue up past two waymarking posts and, 20m/yds further on, fork left on a path. After crossing the *barranco* again, fork right on a path above a restored *cortijo*. Head upriver to join another path (the outward route of Walk 3), just before a *casita* (**5**; **1h52min**). You will climb this path later but, for now, fork left downhill, to take a look at the third bridge, the **Puente Abuchite** (**4**; *P*3;

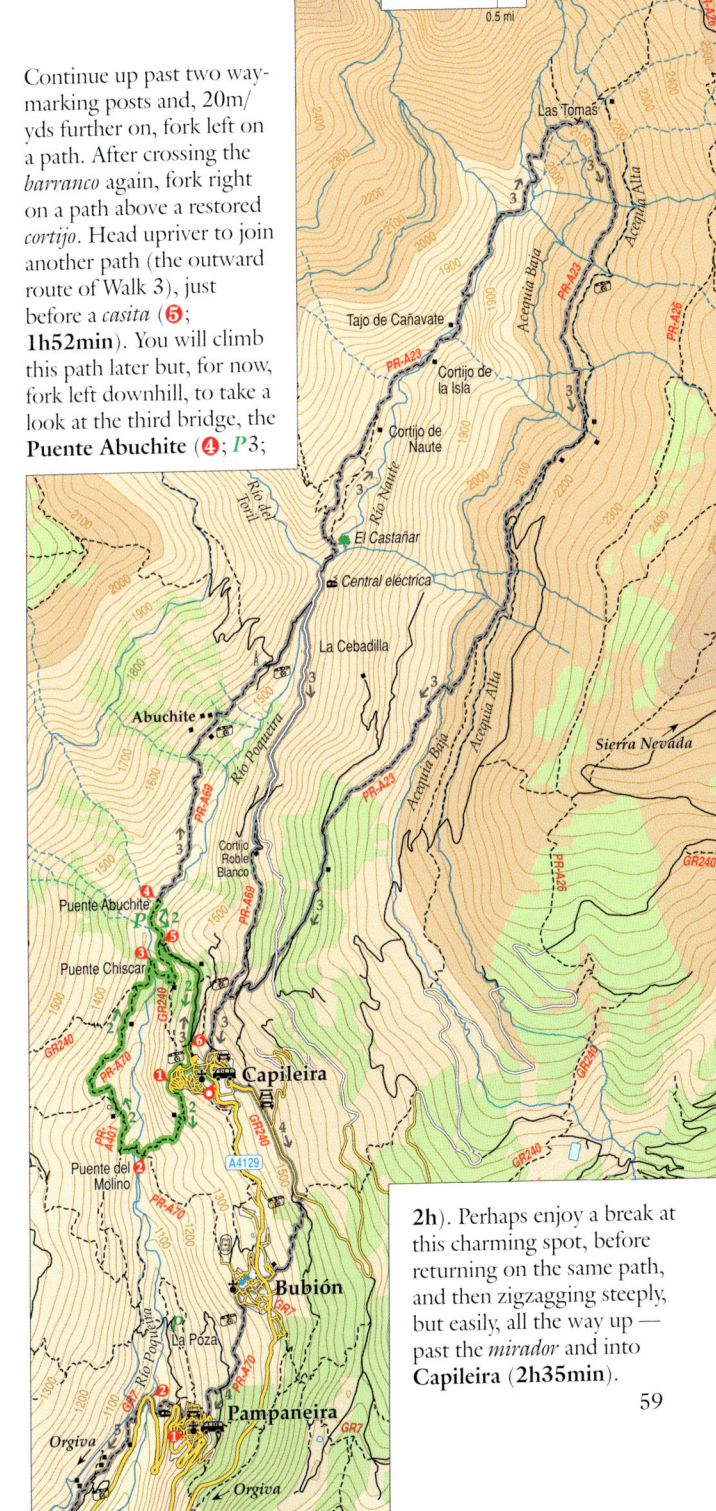

2h). Perhaps enjoy a break at this charming spot, before returning on the same path, and then zigzagging steeply, but easily, all the way up — past the *mirador* and into **Capileira** (**2h35min**).

59

Walk 3: RIO NAUTE, BELOW MULHACEN

See also photo on page 20
Distance: 17km/10.5mi; 6h25min
Grade: ● strenuous but not difficult, with ascents/descents of about 1000m/3300ft overall. The high altitude may cause shortness of breath, so take it easy on the climbs. Be prepared for wet and muddy patches where water drains off the slopes. PR waymarks.
Equipment: See page 51; *walking boots are essential,* trekking pole(s) useful, and take a swimming costume if you wish.
How to get there and return: as Walk 2, page 57.

Short walk: Puente Abuchite (3.2km/2mi; 1h). ● Easy, despite the descent/ascent of 300m/1000ft; equipment as page 51; access as main walk. Follow the main walk to ❷ (28min) and return the same way.

Shorter walk: La Cebadilla (8km/5mi; 2h38min). ● Moderate, with ascents/descents of 320m/1050ft overall; equipment as page 51; access as main walk. Follow the main walk to the BRIDGE reached at 1h38min. Cross it and then pick up the Alternative walk at the 3h16min-point, to return to Capileira (2h38min).

Alternative walk: Cortijo de la Isla (13km/8mi; 4h15min). ● Moderate, with ascents/descents of 470m/1550ft overall; equipment, and access as main walk. Follow the main walk to the **Cortijo de la Isla** (❺; 2h28min). After taking a break, climb back up to the *cortijo* with the *era* and retrace your steps downriver to the INFO BOARDS BY THE BRIDGE (3h06min). Cross this and the next two bridges and follow the dirt road that runs below **La Cebadilla** (❹; 3h16min). It becomes surfaced and climbs gradually. Ignore a track to the right (to Cortijo Roble Blanco; 3h33min); take the next track to the right (at a WAYMARKING POST; 3h38min). Level at first, this track follows an *acequia* which you will see below. Soon the track narrows into a path and passes a couple of *cortijos*. It eventually rises, crosses the *acequia* (now encased in a pipe) and takes you past a restored *cortijo* with a high wall (3h51min). Turn right on the wide track. Then fork right off the track (3h59min) on a path that descends past a little WATER CONTROL HUT. Now pick up the main walk at ❾, to reach Capileira (4h15min).

This excellent walk, full of variety and a naturalist's delight, takes you all the way up the valleys of the Río Poqueira and Río Naute until you are just under the skirts of Mulhacén (3482m/11,420ft), the highest point on the Iberian Peninsula. On your return route, at an altitude of almost 2200m/7200ft, the Veleta ridge seems only a stone's throw away. Always magnificent, these mountains of the Sierra Nevada are dazzlingly beautiful when the sun shines on the lingering snow.

Since this is a long walk, try to set off early, so that you can enjoy a leisurely break at Cortijo de la Isla beside the Río Naute — an idyllic spot, with fine views of Mulhacén. Early birds will also be more likely to catch a view of the *cabra montés*. The ibex (see photo on page 86) roams the western slopes and likes a morning drink from the river.

Walk 3: Río Naute, below Mulhacén 61

Starting from the *ayuntamiento* (**O**) in **Capileira**, follow Walk 2 on page 58 to the Vista Veleta apartments. Then continue on the road to the *mirador* (**❶**), set on the **Eras de Aldeire**. From the *mirador* follow the paved track uphill (yellow/white WAYMARKING POST for PR-A69). The *camino* follows the Poqueira River upstream and, at a WAYMARKING POST tucked away on the right and out of sight (**14min**), winds down to the left on a steep, but stepped, wide and rocky path. You descend to another WAYMARKING POST (**19min**), where Walk 2 comes in from the left and rises to Capileira. Fork right along a level path which passes a stone *casita* and then descends to the river at the **Puente Abuchite** (**❷**; **28min**; *P*3), where the Short walk turns back. Cross the BRIDGE and head right, keeping close to the river as you head upstream. This path, narrow at times, leads up to and round an *era* and old *cortijo* (**41min**), where it levels out for a while. Towering over the head of the valley, Mulhacén comes into view for the first — but by no means the last — time. Also visible are the white houses of La Cebadilla upriver on the opposite bank.

A steep ascent takes you to another *cortijo* (**53min**), where we were once lucky enough to see, crossing our path just ahead, a herd of about a dozen *cabra montés*, making for the seclusion of nearby trees. There are several more *cortijos* along the route, in various stages of repair; most are long-abandoned.

You cross a STREAM where, in mid-October, broom still flowers among the red autumn berries. Head above RUINED ANIMAL SHELTERS and on to another STREAM (**1h21min**). When you reach an *era* at another *cortijo* (**1h23min**), it's worth pausing to take in the views back down the valley.

At a WAYMARKED JUNCTION go straight ahead towards a pylon, passing an info board (in Spanish) about *cortijos*. This area is well cultivated, providing great feeding for small birds; look especially for redstart and larks. Reach the PYLON (**1h28min**), built on an *era*. From here you can see a dirt track below; carry on to where the path meets it at another post or take a short-cut straight down to it. Turn right on the TRACK (**❸**; **1h31min**) and soon, as you round a bend, the views up the valley to Mulhacén are breathtaking.

On the opposite bank is La Cebadilla, a little hamlet built to house the workers at the hydroelectric plant further upriver. Continue to a BRIDGE (**1h41min**) and turn left before crossing it. *(The Shorter walk crosses over to La Cebadilla.)* Now on a narrow concrete road, cross the next bridge at the HYDROELECTRIC PLANT, the point where the Río del Toril and the Río Naute unite to form the **Río Poqueira** (**❹**; **1h44min**).

Follow the dirt track which continues up the **Río Naute**, crosses another bridge and leads to an information panel and WAYMARKING POST (**1h48min**). Take the PR-A23 path which rises in tight bends at the right of the pipe carrying water down to the hydroelectric station. High above the bridge, you go through **El Castañar**, a chestnut grove. The route up the stepped rocks is not difficult, but take it slowly, remembering the altitude. Pass another WAYMARKING POST

(**1h57min**) and enjoy intermittent views of the many waterfalls that cascade down the cliffs opposite. You can regain your breath as the path levels off and heads around a rocky tree-covered mound, before heading upriver again.

Ignore the WAYMARKED ROUTE up to the left (**2h14min**) and continue above the white, isolated but inhabited **Cortijo de Naute**. After the next WAYMARKING POST (**2h19min**) turn down right at yet another *cortijo*, also with an *era*, and start the short descent to the river. When you reach the water, continue upriver and across a little stone BRIDGE, to some ruined stone shelters and a grassy *era*, part of the **Cortijo de la Isla** (❺; **2h28min**). *(The Alternative walk turns back here.)*

From this point you will continue up the valley but, first, take the opportunity to linger here. Set between the clear, fast-flowing river and a lazy stream surrounded by shady trees, you could not wish for more. Yet there *is* more. There is Mulhacén watching over the valley. Enjoy a picnic and perhaps a dip, remembering that although the water may be icy cold, the sun is strong at 1700m (almost 5600ft). Isolated as the area is, we can't guarantee that you will be alone up here.

When you are ready to continue, take the rocky path that runs upstream and winds up to a WAYMARKING POST (**2h33min**). From here the route, somewhat overgrown in places, is marked by wayposts and cairns. Your next target is the *cortijo* you can see directly ahead, high on the slopes of Mulhacén. Cross the river on a stone BRIDGE and continue up the opposite bank past the ruins of the main part of Cortijo de la Isla. Go

Walk 3: Río Naute, below Mulhacén 63

left at a fork, passing a POST at the top of a rise (**2h49min**). Continue downhill, slightly to the right and, as the valley narrows, cross the river again and wind up past another POST (**3h03min**). Water tumbles and gushes all around and, if you look across to the right, you may see icicles dripping from an overhang just before some waterfalls.

The river splits again and, after a steep rise, the path crosses a tributary, making use of convenient rocks, and reaches the MAIN RIVER (**3h16min**), which comes straight off Mulhacén. Winding higher, the path passes another WAYMARKING POST (**3h28min**); at this point you'll hear the Naute (sometimes referred to as the Río Mulhacén on this stretch), raging through the ravine below. Follow waymarks to the **Acequia Baja**, where a narrow path takes you alongside the canal and round to two more WAYMARKING POSTS (**3h33min**). This *acequia*, the lower of a pair, runs down either side of the valley. Because it is fed from the waters that run off the slopes here, this area is known as **Las Tomas** (The Takings), where there is another *cortijo* — the **Cortijo de las Tomas** (**❻**; 2120m; **3h38min**), also known as Cortijo Corral de Pitres).

The main walk continues from here, following the WAYMARKING ARROW uphill, to pass to the right of the *cortijo*. (But if you have really had enough climbing, see the 'Detour route' described overleaf beside the map; **❗**; *possibility of vertigo*) Within a few minutes, another WAYMARKING POST directs you downhill on the PR-A23. (A signpost a few metres higher up points to the Refugio Poqueira — a substantial refuge which is about an hour's walk away, on the slopes directly above the Cortijo de las Tomas. Sitting at 2500m, with a capacity of 87 and every facility a mountaineer could possibly need, it is always open and usually manned. Alternatively, you could follow the *refugio* path up to where it crosses the Acequia Alta, where you would turn right and rejoin the main walk after the 4h20min-point…)

From here, the PR-A23 path descends and continues along a level stretch. Mesmerised by the grandeur of the Veleta ridge, you may miss the next couple of POSTS (**3h52min, 3h62min**). But keep your eyes open beyond them, as you cross a waterfall: we saw an alpine accentor in this spot. The

The Veleta ridge, from the Acequia Alta (about 4h20min into the walk)

path winds up to cross a windswept, grassy slope. As the path undulates past some RUINS AND A POST (**4h09min**), you'll see the Acequia Baja and some of the old *cortijos* it used to serve on slopes below you.

After the next POST (**4h20min**) and a final climb, you come to the **Acequia Alta** (**7**), the upper of the two watercourses. At 2190m/ 7200ft, this is the highest point of

Typical, flower-filled narrow street in Capileira

the walk. Pause for a moment to savour the views shown on pages 62-63 before continuing. The path runs just below the *acequia* but comes right alongside it as it passes below a *cortijo* at the next POST (**4h32min**). Descend to a *casita* and another POST (**4h42min**) and ignore a track going up left to the Sierra Nevada road.

As you proceed now, you will be able to see your outward route snaking along the far side of the valley — and appreciate just how much ground you have covered. It's all downhill from here! You pass a POST (**4h59min**) and then wind down to the Acequia Baja, where there is another POST (**8**; **5h08min**). *(This is where those who followed the 'Detour route' rejoin the main walk.)* Cross the *acequia* and continue the descent. You cross a water pipe (**5h28min**) and enter the pine woods you've been gradually approaching (by another POST; **5h32min**).

Follow the steep path downhill, then go left on a forest track (**5h38min**; POST). Beyond a WATER CONTROL BUILDING, head off right (POST) on a path down through more trees. This brings you on to a forestry road (**5h56min**). Cross the road and wind down the TRACK that starts a few metres to the right. As you draw level with a FARM and an enclosure with several notices over to the right (**6h02min**), look left: a POST marks the start of a path.

Follow the path downhill and turn left past a WATER CONTROL HUT on PR-A69 (**9**; **6h07min**, WAYMARKING POST). Pause to look back and marvel at the 3000m-high ridge that you have been so close to. Then carry on; the *mirador* soon comes into view below, then the roofs of Capileira. At the edge of the village (**6h16min**), go steeply right downhill, past a *fuente* and round to the *ayuntamiento* in **Capileira** (**6h25min**).

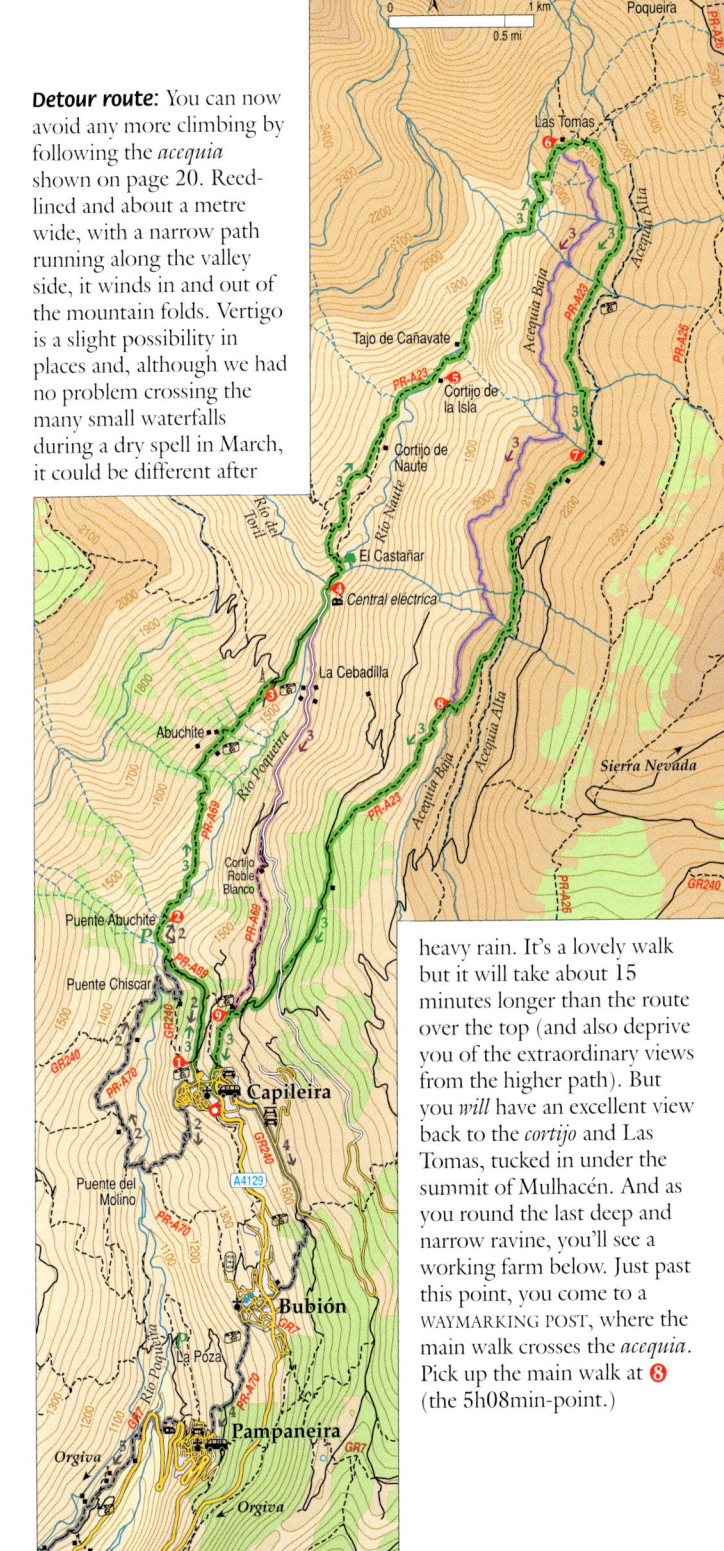

Detour route: You can now avoid any more climbing by following the *acequia* shown on page 20. Reed-lined and about a metre wide, with a narrow path running along the valley side, it winds in and out of the mountain folds. Vertigo is a slight possibility in places and, although we had no problem crossing the many small waterfalls during a dry spell in March, it could be different after heavy rain. It's a lovely walk but it will take about 15 minutes longer than the route over the top (and also deprive you of the extraordinary views from the higher path). But you *will* have an excellent view back to the *cortijo* and Las Tomas, tucked in under the summit of Mulhacén. And as you round the last deep and narrow ravine, you'll see a working farm below. Just past this point, you come to a WAYMARKING POST, where the main walk crosses the *acequia*. Pick up the main walk at ❽ (the 5h08min-point.)

Walk 4: THREE ANDALUSIAN VILLAGES: CAPILEIRA, BUBION AND PAMPANEIRA

See photos on pages 15, 58, 64
Distance: 4km/2.5mi; 1h15min
Grade: ● easy; ascent of 100m/300ft and descent of 430m/1410ft. Some sections are steep and rough underfoot.
Equipment: see page 51.
How to get there and return: 🚌 to/from Pampaneira (the 60km-point on Car tour 1); park in the public car park at the entrance to the village (36° 56.381'N, 3° 21.694'W). From the main road just above the car park, opposite a souvenir shop, catch a bus up to Capileira (Timetable 4; *recheck times!*). The bus will drop you in the centre of Capileira. If you're walking in the morning, you could park in Capileira and catch the bus back from Pampaneira at the end of the walk.

Other walks: This walk could be combined with Walk 5 to make a satisfying and full day out, taking you all the way from Capileira to Órgiva. Or you can create your own walk between any of the seven villages visited on Walks 2-5. Be sure to check bus times before you set out.

This walk, almost all downhill, links the three most typical of the Andalusian villages. Set in the Poqueira Valley, their curious Moorish-style houses are built one above the other in layers and connected by walkways and a system of *acequias*. And everything is whitewashed — even some of the bells in the church at Capileira! Popular with tourists, each village has its share of cafes, bars and handicraft shops. This walk, mostly on long-established mule trails, presents quite a different perspective, allowing you to appreciate how things might have been in the past. Irrigated by the waters that run off the white peaks of Veleta and Mulhacén, the valley is fertile and supports a huge variety of mature trees. The reds and golds of their autumn hues, as they reflect the sunshine, make this a particularly splendid walk around October.

Start the walk at the *ayuntamiento* in **Capileira**, near the bus stop (⭕). This lively place, the last outpost before the Sierra Nevada, has a little museum dedicated to the customs and traditions of the area. Follow the main road (also the GR240, marked red/white on roadside posts) uphill through the village, to the *área recreativa* with picnic tables and benches (❶; **9min**). Here you leave most of the traffic behind. Keep on this road for another nine minutes, to a left-hand bend — years ago the site of a makeshift *mirador* (**18min**) providing a resting spot for village elders on their habitual twice-daily strolls. Continue to a similar spot a little further uphill, just past a line of OVERHEAD CABLES (**21min**), where a path goes down to the right (❷). You're directly above Bubión — a village of dolls' houses under its enormous church.

Turn down this path, *leaving* the GR240, crossing a sealed track in less than 100m. This path is no longer waymarked (it was a PR route when we first walked it).

Although a bit rough, it's a wide and pleasant path descending steeply through a wood of evergreen oaks. It becomes cobbled on passing the first apartments of the **Villa Turistica** holiday complex (**40min**) and leads to the main road through **Bubión** (**43min**).

Bubión's narrow streets form a brilliantly-white labyrinth. Walls and balconies are adorned with colourful pot plants and flowers. Every possible container — buckets, tins, baskets — is used. From here one is quite unaware of the fact that this village advertises itself as a tourist attraction. All evidence of the 'Villa Turística', all the leather work, dried flowers and decorative cloth sold as souvenirs, is confined to the main street at the top of the village.

Cross over and head down through the narrow streets at the right of a bar/café. When you get to the end of Calle Carril, turn right, then first left and make your way to the 16th-century CHURCH (❸; **46min**). Go down to the left of it on the yellow/white marked PR-A70 and turn left, following the sign to Pampaneira. Pass the village wash-house *(lavadero)* and soon find yourself on a steep path, in parts cobbled and stepped. As it levels out there's a good view of the main road twisting, snakelike, on its way down to Pampaneira. There are several small streams running down the slopes, but you should have no problem crossing them unless there has been recent heavy rain.

Pass a fine example of a nicely-restored *era* (**55min**) and continue descending gradually, enjoying the aroma of mint which grows along the route. As you skirt around the terraces, pause to look back to

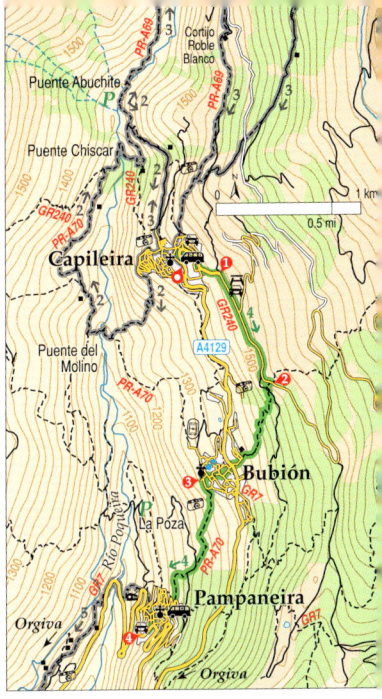

Bubión and the setting shown on page 58, where Capileira stands out against a wonderful backdrop — the ridge between Veleta (3398m) and Mulhacén (3482m). Cross a farm track (**1h03min**) used to transport the produce of the fruit and nut trees that grace the terraces.

As you reach concrete again in **Pampaneira** (**1h09min**), continue down through the village, passing the *lavadero* and *fuente* as you continue down to **Plaza de la Libertad** (**1h13min**), where you'll find the church, bars, handicraft shops and the little local 'Abuela Ili' chocolate factory and shop/museum. Make your way along the left-hand side of the CHURCH to the main road and turn right to the car park (❹; **1h15min**) or, to make a full day of it, perhaps carry on into Walk 5, which would take you all the way to Órgiva.

Walk 5: PAMPANEIRA • SOPORTUJAR • CARATAUNAS • ORGIVA

See also photograph page 15
Distance: 11km/6.8mi; 3h18min
Grade: ● moderate, with some steep sections; ascent of 100m/330ft and descent of 630m/2065ft. Red/white GR7 waymarking to Soportújar.
Equipment: see page 51.
How to get there and return: 🚗 to/from Órgiva; park as near as you can to the PETROL STATION just east of the bridge across the Río Chico (the 45.4km-point on Car tour 1; ⚫; 36° 54.133'N, 4° 25.558'W). Walk back down the main street, towards the bottom of the village, to the bus stop just past the KomoKomo supermarket, in front of the 'Seguridad Social' building. Catch the 11.15 or 13.30 bus (it might be early but is often up to half an hour late) up to Pampaneira and make your way to Plaza de la Libertad, where the church and tourist office are situated.
Other walks: see Walk 4

This walk takes you from village to village along routes which have existed for centuries. You'll pass from fertile mountain slopes to arid wasteland covering old mine workings and from the steep concreted streets of little white villages to the softness of a delightful river valley.

Start in PLAZA DE LA LIBERTAD in **Pampaneira** (❶): walk down the street with a central water channel. Turn left at the bottom and then immediately sharp right, past a sign to Soportújar. This is the GR 7 route, so you'll follow red/white waymarking all the way to Soportújar. Carry on down to the road (where a PR trail marked white/yellow off to the right leads to La Poza; *P*CT1a — see map on page 67) and continue on a path alongside the ELECTRICITY STATION TRANSFORMERS. Meet the road again and follow it to the right, past Pampaneira's HYDROELECTRIC STATION and across the BRIDGE over the Río Poqueira (❷; **13min**). About 100m/yds further on, fork right uphill on a waymarked path. This ancient route to Soportújar, cobbled in places, undulates around the slopes, crossing several gullies and streams en route. At one time the surrounding land was well cultivated, but much is now abandoned.

The good waymarks mean there is little need for directions, but don't miss the point where the path forks left (❸; **38min**; where a right-hand fork leads up to a Buddhist centre). Beyond an inhabited white *cortijo* you'll find stretches of the path overgrown, but it's always clear and runs through chestnut groves. You pass

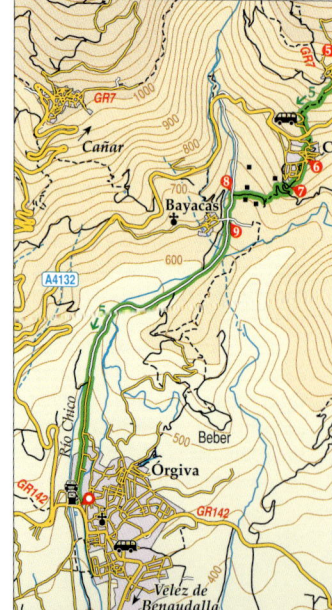

Walk 5: From Pampaneira to Órgiva 69

several ruined *cortijos* and descend to a WAYMARKING POST (**48min**). A bit further on, climb steeply uphill, step over a MANHOLE COVER (**51min**) and then go along a narrow section of path, which is eroded in places. At a junction (**56min**), fork right, to keep uphill, close to a wall. Walk over another MANHOLE COVER and pass a *cortijo* on the left. Cross a gully and walk alongside a WIRE MESH FENCE above a *cortijo* and down into its driveway (**1h05min**, GR POST).

Turn right on a track but, almost immediately, look for the GR marker directing you off left on a little path that runs alongside the fence again. Climb steeply to yet another MANHOLE COVER (**1h10min**) and continue round the slopes, with the left bank falling away steeply. Fork right (**1h16min**) and pass above several more *cortijos*, mostly uninhabited. Notice the CAVE tucked into the right bank after the third of them — there's often washing hanging out at the entrance.

When you emerge on open barren slopes, notice the tiny white **Ermita de Padre Eterno** on the main road below. Turn left when you reach a track (**1h24min**), then go right on the quiet road (**4**; **1h28min**) which comes up from the *ermita*. Soportújar is now visible ahead and, as you walk up the road, the villages of Carataunas and Bayacas come into the picture at the head of the Chico Valley. Clear GR waymarks direct you off the road (**1h34min**), and you head steeply downhill on a rocky path through a desolate area of low growth — the site of former mineral mines. If there are fewer GR markings now, when in doubt, head downwards. Cross a PIPE AT A WATER RESERVOIR (**1h38min**) and, as you continue, notice the village of Cañar perched high on the slopes ahead.

Just after passing the POLIDEPORTIVO (sports facilities; **1h48min**) head up right at a waymark and reach the road. Turn right, noticing Órgiva, your final destination, over to the left. It's still some way to Soportújar, but the road is quiet and the views magnificent from the *mirador* on a bend. After passing the fountain at the entrance to **Soportújar**, you reach the

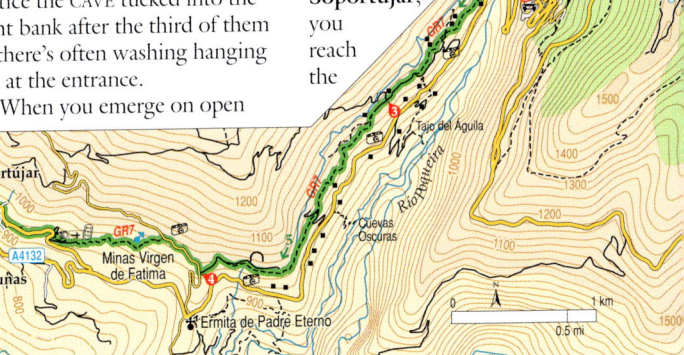

CHURCH (**5**; **2h04min**), where the few buses that bother to come up here stop. The *taberna* makes a pleasant refreshment stop.

The walk continues along the left side of the church on Calle Real. Continue to Calle Estación and turn right, then almost immediately left. Look for the

Órgiva: the church, with impressive twin bell towers, dates from 1580.

'CAMINO DE CARATAUNAS' sign and follow this steep street down to where it becomes a path (actually an old mule trail; **2h10min**). Continue on this; it becomes concrete and brings you to the road (**2h18min**). A DISUSED BUS SHELTER lies just to the left (if you wish to catch the bus from here, you must hail it from outside the bar at the road junction along to the right). Cross the road, going slightly right, and continue down the path, to the CHURCH in **Carataunas** — yet another charming Alpujarran village. The church, *fuente* and tiny Casa Consistorial (with the flags; **❻**; **2h23min**) are worth looking at. The white mulberries that grow around here used to support the worms that, in Arab times, made the village famous for its silk production. The Arabs also exploited the nearby deposits of cobalt and nickel.

Carry on past the Casa Consistorial, then fork left. With walls on either side for a while, this old *camino* takes you out of the village and becomes a track which descends to meet another, concrete track (**❼**; **2h35min**). Turn left and pass LAS MONJAS, a house with colourful gardens, then go through what was once a sizeable hamlet but now has only a few occupied dwellings. Beyond two fenced WATER RESERVOIRS, the square bell tower of the church in Bayacas can be seen just ahead.

Meet a wide dirt road and turn left (**❽**), passing the right turn into Bayacas, a tiny flower-bound village, just a few minutes later (**❾**; **2h41min**). It's well worth a detour and it doesn't take long to explore its steep narrow streets.

The walk continues all the way down the **Río Chico**. Nowadays the river is dry for much of the year, the water being channelled off in *acequias* and used for irrigation. On the way downstream you'll pass stables, a long copse of eucalyptus trees which conceal some little stone cottages and several bridges ranging from the quite substantial to the decidedly rickety (**3h03min**). The track leads into a narrow road with housing (including some rentals) on either side. Olive trees, some centuries old, provide shade for the more delicate crops planted beneath them. The PETROL STATION comes into view ahead and you reach it when you come to the main road through **Órgiva** (**O**; **3h18min**).

WALK 6: VEREDA DE LA ESTRELLA (PATHWAY TO THE STAR)

Distance: 23.5km/14.5mi; 6h50min
Grade: ● strenuous — on account of its length. Ascent/descent of 550m/1800ft, with just one steep section near the start. PR waymarking
Equipment: see page 51.
How to get there and return: 🚗 to/from the Restaurante Maitena at the confluence of the Río Maitena and Río Genil (the 46.2km-point on Detour 2 of Car tour 2). Or take a better road: turn off the main Sierra Nevada road and go through Güéjar Sierra, following signposting to Maitena. Park just past the restaurant (37° 8.961'N, 3° 24.974'W).
Shorter walk: Drive along the narrow old tramline to where it ends by the Estación de San Juan (large car park) and begin the walk there, saving 6.5km/4mi; 1h45min; ● Moderate
Short walk: Estación de San Juan (6.5km/4mi; 1h45min). ● Easy, with a gentle ascent/descent of 120m/395ft; equipment and access as main walk. Follow the main walk to ❷ (56min), cross the bridge to the Estación de San Juan, and return along the tramway.

This well-maintained, well-used and PR-marked path was originally built to serve the iron and copper mines high up the Genil Valley. La Estrella was just the name of one of the mines, but we really did find this to be a most heavenly walk and the path well named. As if mixed woodland, clear-running streams and colourful flowers and berries were not enough, the magnificent 3000m-high ridge of the Sierra Nevada beckons from the head of the valley. To see it all at its best, choose a clear day and bear in mind that the sun won't be in a suitable position for photographing the high peaks until around 3pm. Being an out-and-back walk, you are not obliged to finish it but, if you do cut it short, make sure you at least go to the Mirador del Genil (1h54min), for views you will never forget.

Start out just past the Restaurante Maitena (⭕), at the CONFLUENCE OF THE **Maitena and Genil rivers**; the restautant is housed in the old **Maitena tram station**. Continue walking upstream along the road (at this point built over the OLD TRAMLINE). You can either stay on the road and walk through two short TUNNELS, or take the path off to the right after about 100m and avoid the tunnels. Some 15m after the path rejoins the road, the road itself crosses the river as the 'main' road (the route of Detour 2 in Car tour 2). But turn left at the fork before the road bridge on a lane signposted to the BARRANCO DE SAN JUAN and VEREDA ESTRELLA (among others) — the surfaced continuation of the old TRAMLINE (**13min**).

You go through a TUNNEL immediately, then pass the old **El Charcón station** and go through another short TUNNEL which lies between the Restaurante Los Castaños and Mesón Restaurante El Charcón on the opposite side of the Río Genil. Cross the BRIDGE

(**26min**) to the Café Bar Chiquito and continue, with the river now on your left. Just before the tramway goes over a bridge then through a very short tunnel, little more than an archway, take the clear path, with yellow and white PR WAYMARKINGS, which goes up to the right (❶; **32min**). This is the start of the **Vereda de la Estrella**, which you will follow all the way up the Genil Valley and beyond it.

Rise above the river and cross a stream (where you may see dipper), and pass along the back of a WATER CONTROL BUILDING (**46min**). Cross another stream and go up past ruined alpine-style chalets and along a FENCE (**53min**) surrounding chalets still in use. Wind downhill and cross a WOODEN BRIDGE over the **Barranco de San Juan**, an excellent picnic spot (❷; **56min**; P6). The site of the old **Estación de San Juan** (now a restaurant), is to your left on the far side of the Río Genil, at the END OF THE TRAMWAY. (*The Short walk crosses to the station here and returns along the surfaced tramway.*)

From the *barranco*, go up the slope on a wide path; it continues to follow the Río Genil upstream, winding steeply uphill. After emerging from the trees, the path levels out, then undulates lazily towards the mountains. You will pass a huge chestnut tree; its branches and gnarled contorted trunk and roots overhang the path. Affectionately known as **El Abuelo** ('the Grandfather'; ❸; **1h31min**), it is said to be the most massive tree in the valley. On the slopes on the far side of the river are the almond groves which used to be tended from the old *cortijo* high on the hill, now in ruins. We flushed several groups of red-legged partridge here.

Ignore a path going down left to cross the river (**1h33min**) and another, very faint path (**1h53min**), which climbs to the

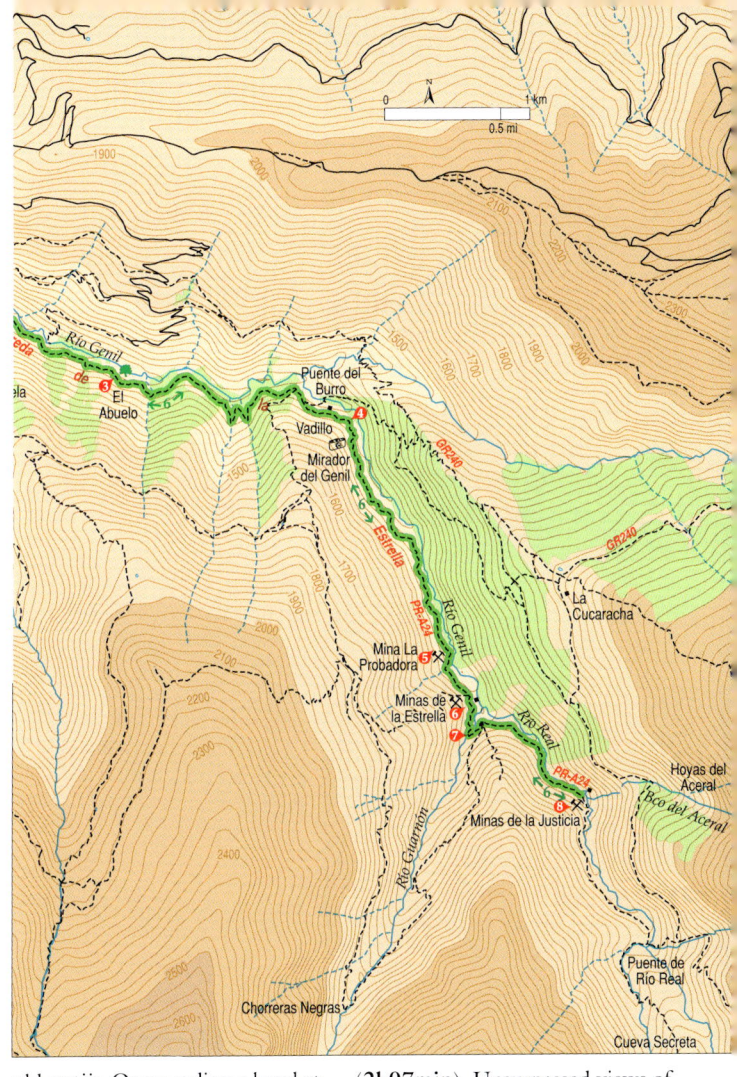

old *cortijo*. On rounding a bend at a rocky PROMONTORY (**1h58min**), you overlook the confluence of two *barrancos*. But resist the temptation to stop for a break here; continue ahead, passing a clear path down to the Vadillo mountaineering hut by the Puente del Burro (popular starting point for an assault on the north face of the Sierra Nevada ridge). Soon after, round a bend, you come to the **Mirador del Genil** (**4**), with PR MARKINGS on one of the rocks (**2h07min**). Unsurpassed views of Alcazaba (3366m) and Mulhacén (3482m) make *this* the place to pause.

Beyond the *mirador,* the path undulates in the setting shown overleaf, eventually coming to ruins of old houses at the **Mina La Probadora** (**5**; **2h44min**), the best known of the mines in the Sierra Nevada. The mining tunnel still exists today, extending deep into the mountainside. A few slaty steps take you up and across a

Stone bridge over the Río Guarnón (top) and path beyond the Mirador del Genil, with Mulhacén in the background (below)

Cortijo and **Minas de la Estrella** (**6**; **3h03min**), in an open grassy spot where another tunnel remains as evidence of past activity. This site overlooks the confluence of the Río Real, which drains Veleta, and the Río Guarnón which drains Alcazaba and Mulhacén. The two unite to form the Genil. Cross the STONE BRIDGE (**7**) over the Guarnón (shown left), before heading up the Real.

The path, now narrower but still clear, climbs to more ruins, the **Minas de la Justicia** (**8**; **3h31min**). Just beyond these, take the steep path on the left, down to the the lower mine houses closer to the river. You can reach the water's edge from here (**3h33min**).

Although the main path continues for a further half hour or more to Cueva Secreta, another base camp for major climbs to the peaks, and another, steep and narrow path to the east rejoins our outgoing route (see map), our walk ends at this excellent picnic spot, to allow plenty of time for the return.

Retrace your steps past Cortijo de la Estrella (**4h08min**). Then remember to fork down right where the two little paths go up left (**4h13min**). Pass the mine houses (**4h21min**), the *mirador* (**4h53min**), the path to the Vadillo hut (**4h59min**), and El Abuelo (**5h32min**). When you reach the **Estación de San Juan** (**6h02min**), either retrace your steps or cross the bridge to the old tramline, to return to the **Restaurante Maitena** (**6h50min**).

WATERFALL, and the path climbs steeply for a while. Take it easy, remembering that you are walking at altitude. A couple of narrow paths come off the mountain from the right, just before a bend where the Veleta ridge appears ahead. Descend to ruins below, the

Walk 7: BELOW THE COLLADO DE LAS SABINAS

Distance: 9.5km/5.9mi; 2h30min
Grade: ● moderate, given the high altitude — take it easy. Ascent/descent of only about 300m/1000ft. Some yellow/white PR waymarking
Equipment: see page 51.
How to get there and return: 🚗 to/from the 38km-point on Detour 2 of Car tour 2 (0.8km northeast of the Sierra Nevada Visitor Centre); park off the road on the hairpin bend to the left, where a track goes off to the right (37° 8.210'N, 3° 25.719'W).

Shorter walks
1 Barranco de los Tejos (4.6km/2.9mi; 1h15min). 🔵 Easy, with a gentle ascent/descent of 100m/330ft — but be aware of the altitude. Equipment and access as the main walk. Follow the main walk over the stream in the Barranco de los Tejos and past the chain (❸; 35min). Continue till you are in sight of the farm and then retrace your steps back to your car.

2 Casa de Prado Redondo (5.5km/3.4mi; 1h47min). ● Moderate because of the altitude, with an ascent/descent of 300m/1000ft. Equipment and access as above. Follow the main walk to the uphill path (❶) and turn right, picking up the walk at the 1h02min-point. From the Casa de Prado Redondo, just retrace your steps.

Fresh mountain air and the fragrance of pines make this walk an exhilarating experience — with the added attraction of seeing the high peaks of the sierra, snow-covered for about 10 months of the year, in all their glory.

Start out by going down the TRACK (**O**), following the yellow and white waymarks of the PR-A19 on LOW WOODEN POSTS. Almost immediately the 3000m ridge of the Sierra Nevada comes into view ahead. Ignore a track to the left (**3min**) and start climbing. As the track bends right (**8min**), the serrated crags of Alcazaba (3366m) appear, while the lesser crags below the Collado de las Sabinas tower above you to the right. At a JUNCTION (**11min**), take the widest track, furthest to the left, through shady pines (the middle track rises to a cabin, *P*7a). Cross the **Río Seco** and notice the variety of trees that line the route — including oak, juniper and hawthorn. Fork right (**13min**) and soon reach a 'BALCONY', where a *finca* lies just below (**16min**; *P*7b). Just 20m/yds further on, take note of the path up to the right (❶); you will be climbing it later in the walk; continue along the track.

The mountains at the head of the valley loom larger and the terraces of the Genil Valley come into view just before the track crosses a running stream through the **Barranco de los Tejos** (❷; **25min**). After passing a chained entrance to orchards on the left, the track runs level across the top of terracing. Some 400m after crossing the Tejos, there is a CHAIN across the track (❸; **35min**). The land ahead is private, but you can continue a little further uphill for closer views of the mountains. When the FARM comes into sight below (**39min**), take a last look around then retrace your steps to the uphill path at ❶ (**1h02min**); it is now on your left.

At a T-junctiom, turn left on a track (**1h07min**) and then (after 150m fork right at the left-hand

The Casa de Prado Redondo, backed by the rocky outcrop

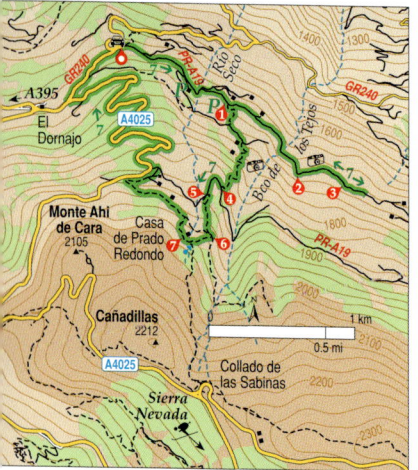

track, go left on a pleasant PATH (**5**; *not signposted*) which climbs steadily through low pines. Kestrel hover above, perhaps eyeing the partridge you are likely to flush from the low vegetation.

When you meet another, somewhat eroded, track (**6**; **1h33min**), turn left and then (after 50m) take the next path to the right (SIGNPOSTED; **1h36min**). Soon after passing under the cables, reach a JUNCTION with a rocky outcrop ahead. The ruined house shown above left, the **Casa de Prado Redondo** (**7**), is off to the right (**1h39min**) — before reaching it, you pass a *fuente*.

Now walk behind the *casa*, and continue down the path below the rock face. After a while it becomes a track (the eroded track you followed briefly earlier in the walk); below is one of the major tracks you crossed earlier. Follow the track down to a parking bay and turn right on the road. There are plenty of short-cuts if you want to avoid the zigzags but, keeping to the road, you approach the **Visitor Centre** (**2h24min**) and turn right just before it, back to your car (**2h30min**).

side of a ruin (**1h09min**). Zigzag uphill towards a pine wood under the crags. Pass to the left of the pines (**1h14min**) and pause to look around. Over to the left, the main sierra ridge rises majestically beyond the deep gully formed by the Barranco de los Tejos where you have just been. Behind you lies the Genil Valley, focal point of Walk 6.

When you meet a signposted TRACK (**1h24min**), turn right, heading along the crags you saw from below. Above you can see electricity cables and the pointed peak of Monte Ahi de Cara. After walking just over 200m along this

Walk 8: TOMA DEL CANAL

Distance: 14.5km/9mi; 4h23min
Grade: ● moderate, with ascents/descents of 550m/1800ft overall, including some sustained climbing from Toma del Canal. Yellow/white waymarking of the PR-A21. The main and alternative walks should not be attempted just after heavy rainfall, as the Barranco del Búho may be subject to flash floods.
Equipment: see page 51; *walking boots with ankle support essential*
How to get there and return:
🚗 car to/from the Fuente del Hervidero (the 10km-point on Detour 1 of Car tour 2; 37° 5.260'N, 3° 31.969'W). You *could* start this walk at ❶ (the 15min-point, where there is a parking area and the waymarking begins). But we like filling up water bottles at the *fuente* before setting off and relaxing with a beer or late lunch at this country restaurant on the return.

Short walk: Puente de los Siete Ojos (6.2km/3.8mi; 1h20min). 🔵 Easy, with ascents/descents of 170m/560ft overall. Access and equipment as main walk, but trainers will do. Follow the *Alternative walk* to the 40min-point ('Bridge of the Seven Eyes') and return the same way.

Alternative walk: La Cortijuela — Collado de Trevenque — Collado de las Chaquetas (17km/10.5mi; 4h07min). ● Moderate, with ascents/descents of 540m/1775ft overall. Access and equipment as main walk. Follow the main walk almost to ❶ (the 15min-point), but instead of going up on to the raised car park, continue on the GRAVEL ROAD up the Huenes Valley (yellow/white waymarked PR-A20) and past a chain barrier. As the valley closes in (34min) ignore the path that goes down to an *acequia* above the river, and reach the **Puente de los Siete Ojos** (Bridge of the Seven Eyes; ❷; 40min; *P*8). Follow the road as it crosses the bridge and climbs steadily with just the odd zigzag. A track comes off Cerro Gordo from the left just before **La Cortijuela**, a forestry house (❸; 1h36min). This has a charming botanic garden run by the Junta de Andalucía.

From here the road swings round to the right and becomes little more than a track. Thus far the terrain has been lightly wooded, but it now thickens as you pass behind Trevenque's triangular peak. At the **Collado del Trevenque** (❹; 2h01min) a path goes up the ridge, heading for the summit. Forego that pleasure and continue up to the WATERSHED between the Huenes and Dilar valleys (2h08min).

The terrain then opens out as you begin to descend. The Dilar Valley, overlooked by the rugged crags of Los Alayos, is visible below before you round a bend and come upon an open grassy meadow with farm buildings (❺; 2h20min), the **Collado de las Chaquetas** — known locally as a goat supermarket. Replenish your water bottles at the *fuente* on the approach, then continue on the track which bears right, up towards a pine wood, before starting to descend again. The track sweeps round a hairpin bend to the left as it crosses the bed of the **Barranco de Aguas Blanquillas** (2h33min). Just after the bend, take a wide path off to the right (WAYMARKS). You join the main walk at ❻ (the 2h49min-point). Follow it back to the **Fuente del Hervidero** (4h07min).

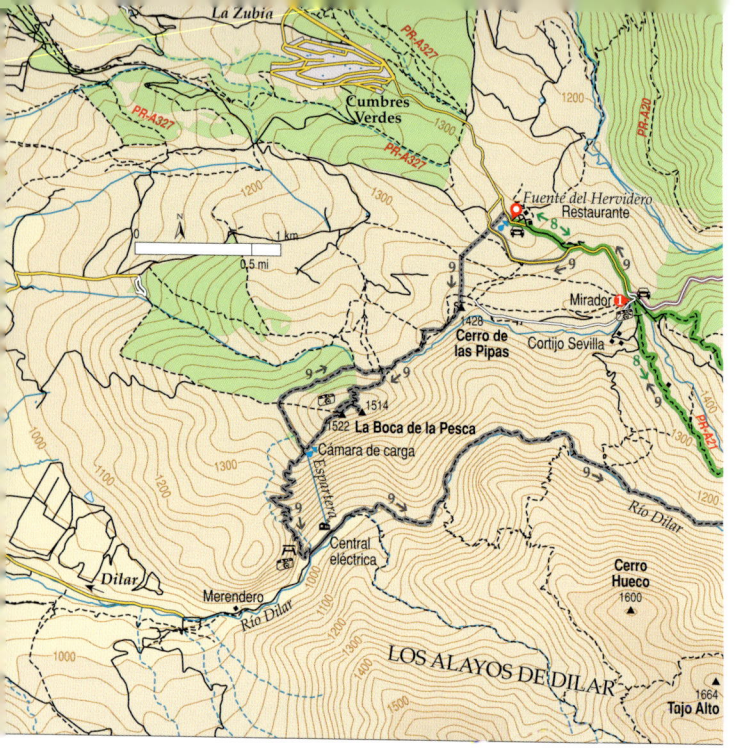

Toma del Canal is the point where water is drawn from the Río Dilar and pumped into the Canal de la Espartera. This canal then transports it around the hillsides to a water tank on the slopes of the Boca de la Pesca, only to be dropped back into the Dilar Valley further downstream, to fuel the turbines at the power station (Walk 9). This is an enjoyable walk at any time, but we particularly enjoy it in autumn when the trees are at their colourful best.

Start out from the CAR PARK at the **Fuente del Hervidero** (⭕). Follow the narrow road into the Huenes Valley. Pass under cables and go up to the right, past some notice boards and onto a raised area, the **Mirador del Canal de la Espartera** (also called Mirador de los Alayos; ❶; **15min**), where there is another CAR PARK. Across the Dilar Valley are the rugged crags of the Alayos de Dilar and to the right, towering over the old Cortijo Sevilla and a couple of other buildings, is the pointed Boca de la Pesca. You'll be seeing more of this twin-peaked mountain later on.

Three routes start here, and you are following the PR-A21, which heads down to the right. The walk will return by the upper track on the left. We used to like to take the middle path, alongside the the narrow but substantial **Canal de la Espartera**, but it is not officially allowed now. (If you *do* follow the path alongside the *canal*, be sure to take the narrow path down to the main PR-A21 after about 750m.

The route undulates pleasantly in and out of trees as the delightful

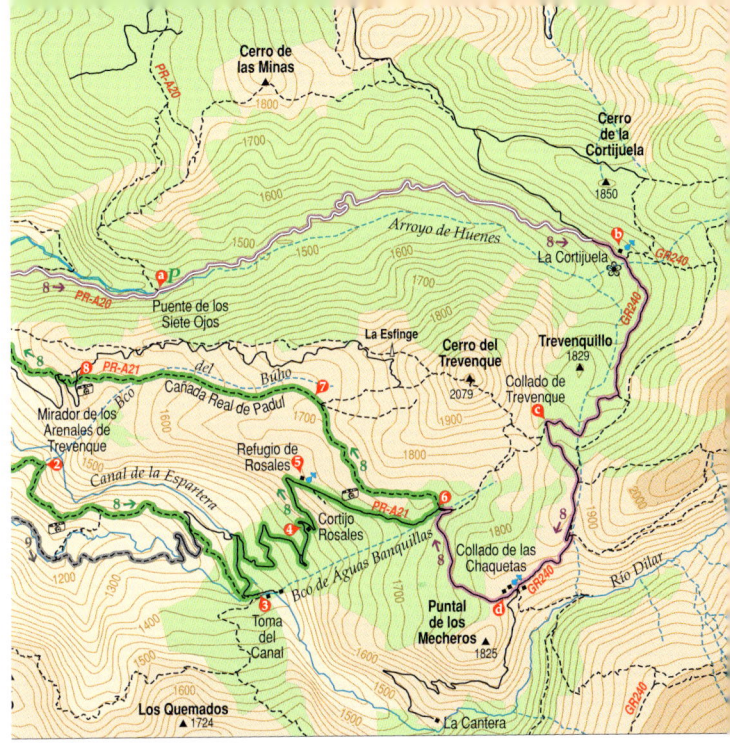

path contours the hillsides above the **Río Dilar**. Rounding the tall cliffs that circle the **Barranco del Búho** (❷; **50min**), the sound of water filters up from far below. Further on, from a rocky *mirador* with a PR SIGNPOST (**1h06min**) you'll see a waterfall in the tree-lined Dilar Valley and perhaps witness a golden eagle on the hunt. The path continues gently downhill, and the countryside opens out as you draw closer to the river.

Then you ascend a little, through pines, noticing the canal up on the left. Ignore a track down to the river (**1h33min**); your path brings you to the river not long after, at **Toma del Canal** (❸; **1h49min**), with a couple of buildings and a tank to regulate the amount of water in the canal. Lining the river there's a tangle of exuberant vegetation.

Your onward trail, WAYMARKED, is a long and demanding ascent on a JEEP TRACK, between hawthorns, holm oaks, cherry trees and pines. But first you will want to explore this beautiful spot. A narrow path leads a little way along the river to another building where there are more fig trees, and you have a chance to dip your fingers in the icy clear water. The only disturbance is likely to be the squawking of jays.

Ascending, after crossing the *canal,* you reach a flat area above a now-defunct mountain refuge hut, the **Cortijo de Rosales** (❹; **2h13min**). The surrounding ground, churned up by wild boar, is much appreciated by red-legged partridge. Carry on up the forestry track which winds steeply around the *cortijo,* and prepare yourself for breathtaking views. You pass a *fuente* with icy water at a new

View to Boca de la Pesca (on the right) from the Canal de la Espartera. Walk 9 would take you over 'Fish-Mouth'.

stone MOUNTAIN HUT set in a fantastic spot overlooking the mountains and valley (**Refugio de Rosales**; ❺; **2h26min**); an info board here — unfortunately only in Spanish — discusses the dolomitic rock formations, the endemic plant life and the soil.

Carry on climbing again to another level area, where the **Barranco de Aguas Blanquillas**, frozen in winter, goes back to the right. Take the narrow path which rises steeply to the left and, within a few metres, meet another signposted path (❻; **2h49min**). *(The Alternative walk comes in here from the right.)* Turn left on the 'Cañada Real de Padul al Pico Veleta', passing another info board.

This undulating path runs above your outward route, so the Dilar River is now far away down on the left. Deviate for a moment to a crest, the highest point on the walk (1760m/5775ft): from this *mirador* you can see all the peaks which form the crest of the Alayos. Ahead are the Arenales, gravel 'rivers' forming sandy-coloured slopes. Head for them. On coming to a saddle (**3h10min**), you'll see a dirt road cutting across the hillside straight ahead; you will cross it later. Your path is heavily trodden by goats, and you may have to barge through the multicoloured herd as it blocks your way.

If you are lucky you may see a *cabra montés* silhouetted on top of the ridge. You will definitely see the crags of Trevenque up to the right and, below them, to the left, the rock formation they call La Esfinge (The Sphinx). From the saddle the path drops into a wide gravelly *barranco*, the top end of the **Barranco del Búho** (❼).

Follow this easy route downhill via the **Mirador de los Arenales de Trevenque** (❽), with another info panel about the origins of the *arenales*. Beyond yet another info panel you leave the Cañada Real for a signposted path to the right and a somewhat vertiginous zigzag descent back to the car park at ❶ (**4h06min**) and the **Fuente del Hervidero** (**4h23min**).

9 BOCA DE LA PESCA

See also photo opposite
Distance: 15.3km/9.5mi; 5h50min
Grade: ●❗ strenuous, with ascents/descents of 740m/2430ft overall. You must be sure-footed for the steep gravelly descent and have a head for heights. Expect river crossings and be aware of the altitude. Informal signposting
Equipment: see page 51; *additionally: boots with ankle support, compass, towel, extra socks, plenty of water; optional plimsolls for river crossings.*
How to get there and return:
🚗 car to/from the Fuente del Hervidero, as Walk 8 on page 77
Short walks: equipment as on page 51; access as main walk

1 *Sierra Nevada view* (2.5km/ 1.6mi; 50min). ● Easy; ascent/descent of 145m/475ft. Follow the main walk to ❶ (the 25min-point on **Cerro de las Pipas**) and return the same way.

2 *Boca de la Pesca summit* (4km/2.5mi; 1h50min). ● Moderate, with ascent/descent of 250m/820ft. Follow the main walk to ❷ (the 58min-point on the higher summit) and retrace steps.

Alternative walk: Dilar Valley (10km/6.2mi; 4h04min). ●❗ Strenuous, with ascents/descents of 640m/2100ft overall. You must be sure-footed for the steep gravelly descent and have a head for heights. Access and equipment as main walk (less towel and socks). Follow the main walk to ❺ (the 2h09min-point by the **Río Dilar**). After resting and exploring, return by the same path (it starts between the last ELECTRICITY POST and a CONCRETE BLOCK) as far as ❹ (the WATER TANK — *Cámara de carga*; 3h08min). Cast a last look back into the Dilar Valley and take the path to the left, which skirts the hillside. It soon crosses a firebreak and runs through the trees along the bottom edge of the wood. Follow it above the Canal de la Espartera, rejoin your outward path and, turning left, follow it under the crags of Cerro de las Pipas (❶; 3h45min). Head downhill through the scrub and fields to the **Fuente del Hervidero**.

At 1522m (almost 5000ft), aptly-named Boca de la Pesca (Fish-Mouth), is no mean mountain. But although it provides the focal point for this walk, there is much more to enjoy. The upriver trek is delightful at any time of year but, after significant rainfall, when the path at times disappears under water, it becomes quite an adventure!

Start out with your back to the **Fuente del Hervidero** and RESTAURANT (⭕). Ahead, locate the distinctive rocky outcrop shown on page 84, Cerro de las Pipas (1428m), your first objective. Cross a ploughed field, then the road, and then another field; there's no definite track, but you'll see where folk have trodden in the clay soil previously. Cross a track into another field and cut left towards the hillside. Leaving the fields behind, make your way up the slopes through low scrub, herbs and lavender. Head for the right-hand side of the crags, crossing a couple of paths en route. From the crest, not far below the summit of **Cerro de las Pipas** (❶; **25min**), the 3000m ridge of the Sierra Nevada is awe-inspiring. Boca de la Pesca, not as high but nevertheless imposing, is directly

ahead, and your onward path is clear, running towards the woods on its northwest face.

After crossing a small saddle, choose the path which you see leading all the way to the edge of the wood, meeting the wood a little more than halfway up the line of trees (**48min**). Follow it up the edge of the wood for a short distance, then turn left and zigzag up through trees. Just below the summit the path meets a FIREBREAK. To the left, you see the top of the manned lighthouse-like FIRE WATCH STATION (**2**) and on the far side of the firebreak is the path you will later take downhill: having located it, continue to the top, the higher of the twin summits of **Boca de la Pesca** (1518m; **3**; **58min**).

Then return to the fire-watch station on the lower summit (1513). From a stretch of low wall you can safely admire the panoramic views. To the left, across the *boca*, is the sharp twin peak with trig point, where you have just been, and a lone holm oak. Behind it, rising majestically in the distance, is Trevenque (2079m), the dominating peak of this immediate region. Straight ahead, to the southeast, are the Alayos de Dilar, a line of rocky crags overlooking the Dilar Valley. Towering at the head of the valley is Pico Veleta (3398m), second highest peak of the Sierra Nevada. Behind you, the Vega de Granada extends beyond La Zubia and on to Granada itself. From the left-hand end of the wall, locate your next target, the Central Eléctrica de Dilar, a hydroelectric power station far below on the banks of the river.

Once ready for the descent, go back to the other end of the wall and pass between some trees, to join the path you identified on the way up. It will take you all the way to the river. It is very steep and stony and *requires care*. It passes to the right of the *Cámara de carga* (**4**; **1h18min**), A WATER CONTROL BUILDING where the Canal de la Espartera (Walk 8) ends. From here the water is dropped back into

The Dilar Valley — from the viewpoint near the end of the walk; below: Alayos de Dilar

the valley to power the turbines of the hydroelectric station.

The path crosses the canal just below the building and starts you on the second part of the descent. It's still rough, and stony and steep in places but, if you ignore the almost-vertical short cuts and keep to the longer, gentle zigzags, you'll find the going much easier than on the upper section. Listen and look out for ravens, choughs and crag martins. Soon after passing alongside some retaining walls and crossing a small stream (**1h52min**), you come to a promontory with marvellous views.

Set off again and reach the foot of the path at the DIRT TRACK (**5**; **2h09min**) that runs along the river from Dilar, a village 5km to the right. This is a glorious spot to rest and perhaps picnic and explore a little. To the right, picnic benches sit among the trees by the riverside and about 1km further on is a *merendero*, open at weekends. To the left are the power station buildings and some delightful areas close to the water. In the mornings and evenings *cabra montés* come down from the slopes to drink here.

Continuing the main walk, turn left on the track. *(The Alternative walk climbs back up the path.)* After passing the **Central eléctrica** (**6**), go a metre/3ft or so up to the left, onto an *acequia*. Walk along it for about 100m, then pick up a path heading upstream. From here you may have to take off boots and socks up to eight times, in order to cross the river! Although it is not very wide, it can be very fast-flowing and icy cold. We have allowed extra time for crossings, but in the dry season there may be

no problem at all. Essentially, the path just continues upstream, with crossings coming in pairs to cut off bends in the river. There are numbered WAYMARKING POSTS, usually at crossing points.

Left: approaching Cerro de las Pipas

The valley closes in somewhat and you find yourself walking through trees, with tall cliffs to either side and incredible rock formations ahead. Emerging from the trees, the path becomes stony, running a few metres above river level (**2h44min**) and climbing to a WAYMARKED ELECTRICITY POST (**2h50min**). A level stretch takes you across the slopes and through an open area where saffron crocuses blow gently in the breeze. The path then heads past another WAYMARKER and straight up a short gully in the rock face. Steps have been hewn out to make it easy, and you soon reach another electricity post at the top. Whatever the season this is a picturesque spot, always colourful with flowers or berries.

Descend to the waterside again (**3h**) where a further WAYMARKING POST directs you right, to negotiate another two river crossings (**3h04min**). On dry land again, as you cross a shallow, gravelly *barranco* (**3h20min**), look up to the left and see the top of a tower.

This is adjacent to the Cortijo Sevilla which you will pass later on. At the head of a second *barranco* a few distinctive pinnacles top a line of cliffs. There are then four more river crossings in quick succession, a 'CAZA' (HUNTING) SIGN after the first (**3h30min**).

With pines standing erect on top of the ridge up to the left, the valley opens up to the right (**4h05min**), and the path passes beneath cables close to WAYMARKING POST 5. Where two valleys meet (**4h14min**), with a wide gravelly *barranco* ahead and to the right, you can either cross the river twice more (but it's much deeper and faster up here), or go up left and clamber, keeping high, round a huge boulder. We prefer the latter option. Back at river level, pick up the path again and pass WAYMARKING POST 6 (**4h35min**) as you go up a slope, now bearing left on a track, away from the river.

Meet a wide earthen PATH (**❼**; **4h49min**) which runs almost level along the hillside and turn left. (Walk 8 started out on this path en route for Toma del Canal.) Pause at a rocky *mirador* for a different view of the Boca de la Pesca and, after rounding the cliffs of the **Barranco del Búho** (**❽**; **5h04min**), climb gradually, to pass to the right of the **Cortijo Sevilla** (**❾**; **5h25min**). Continue up to a raised area used as a car park. Drop down to the Huenes Valley road (**5h30min**) and turn left. Cut off on a track to the right (**5h38min**); it takes you back to the **Fuente del Hervidero** (**5h50min**).

Walk 10: CUEVA DE NERJA • LA CIVILA • CORTIJO MOLINERO • CUEVA DE NERJA

Distance: 14km/8.7mi; 4h46min (about 1h less if you omit La Civila, 200m/650ft uphill)

Grade: ● strenuous, with an ascent (sometimes steep)/descent of 630m/2400ft overall. Some rough walking in dry river beds which could be subject to flash floods after rain.

Equipment: see page 51; *boots with ankle support are essential, and long trousers are advisable for the last section of the main walk.*

How to get there and return: 🚗 or 🚌 (Timetable 3a, 3b) to/from the Cueva de Nerja (starting point of Car tour 3). Large car park (36° 45.694'N, 3° 50.853'W)

Short walk: Barranco de la Coladilla (6.5km/4mi; 1h42min). ● Moderate, with ascent/descent of 185m/600ft (including a short clamber up rocks). Equipment as page 51; access as main walk. Follow the main walk to ❷ (the 45min-point). Continue straight ahead (slightly left) and, a couple of minutes later, take the rough track which turns back to the left and leads you down into the **Barranco de la Coladilla** (52min).

Pines and eucalypts shade you from the sun and, underfoot, deep runnels have been forged by storm water. To either side, tall cliffs are pitted with caves and are home to families of crag martins. In spring, broom provides occasional eye-catching splashes of colour, and at any time of year you'll feel peaceful as you stroll along.

Just before the *barranco* veers left and about 100m before a track heads up and out of it (1h20min), take the path heading sharply back to the left and crossing the *barranco*. Follow this path to your outward track (1h27min), where you turn right and return to your car (1h42min).

Alternative walk: El Pinarillo — Fuente del Esparto — Collado de los Apretaderos (12.6km/7.8mi; 3h27min). ● Moderate, with ascents/descents of 430m/1410ft overall. Equipment and access as main walk. Follow the main walk to ❷ (the 45min-point) and continue straight ahead (slightly left; signed 'EL PINARILLO 2KM'). A couple of minutes later, you pass the point where the Short walk turns left; continue up the track. If any reforestation is underway — as it was when we were last there — see how the young trees are protected from the nibbling of the *cabra montés*. Shortly after a series of DAM WALLS to the left, cross a small *barranco* and soon reach **El Pinarillo** (ⓐ; 1h11min) on the left, a *zona recreativa* with a tiny botanic garden.

You will return here later but, for now, carry on, noticing the rugged crags at the end of the Cielo ridge on the right before going past a barrier. Cross the **Barranco de la Coladilla** (1h26min), beyond which the track bends left and runs back along the opposite side of the *barranco* from El Pinarillo. Ignore a track coming off the mountain from the right (1h31min). Bearing left, you pass old *cortijo* ruins. Pause to look back, to a tremendous view of the mountains unfolding into the distance.

Contour above the *barranco* and reach the **Fuente del Esparto** (ⓑ; 1h33min), shaded by eucalyptus and palms, where hopefully you can fill your bottles from the spring on the right (*warning:* the spring is sometimes dry). As El Pinarillo comes into view again (1h37min) you'll see the helipad and reservoir used for fire control and, closer to the picnic area, an old *era*.

Ignore a track to the left (1h42min) which zigzags back to El Pinarillo and start climbing again on a track lined in spring with rock roses and the little yellow tufts of *santolina* (lavender cotton). After a steep concrete section of path, you reach the **Collado de los Apretaderos** (●; 550m; 1h48min). Walk 11 joins here. Look out straight ahead to fantastic views over the Chillar Valley. Then look left and notice two paths going slightly uphill. Just before these and to their left, is a downhill path marked by a POST WITH A WHITE ARROW. This old mule trail is initially a bit tricky but, as it heads right, it levels out and cuts gradually downhill through low scrub. Cross a TRACK (2h01min) and follow the path as it bears left downhill between large rocks. Crossing the *barranco*, reach a flat area, formerly a sports pitch. Take the steep path up to the right, to the picnic benches at **El Pinarillo** (2h11min). Walk over to the track and turn right: it will take you all the way back to the Cueva de Nerja car park.

Being so easily accessible from the coast, the GR/PR track above the Barranco de la Coladilla is busy on Sundays and *fiestas*, since El Pinarillo, La Civila and the Fuente del Esparto are popular picnic spots. So tackle these walks on a weekday, when you can enjoy the glorious countryside in peace. Note, too, that this track is motorable and can be very dusty; you can avoid part of it by following the Barranco de la Coladilla (the return route for the Short walk) *up*hill as well as down — follow the route highlighted in violet on the map.

Start the walk from outside the **Cueva de Nerja** CAR PARK (●): walk up the wide track signposted to the ÁREA RECREATIVA, heading towards the hills. This track, which served the many iron mines higher up on the mountains, curves left and passes a post with red/white GR waymarking and then a large PARQUE NATURAL sign. You climb gradually, with the **Barranco de Maro** on your left. Pass a track off to the right and notice a SMALL PATH (●; **19min**) emerging from the left — the Short walk comes out of the *barranco* here and heads

Statue of a cabra montés *(Spanish ibex) at the El Pinarillo zona recreativa (Alternative walk)*

Walk 10: Circuit based on the Cueva de Nerja

back down the track. The pines on either side become more dense, but the track is still in full sun.

At a clear junction (signposted simply 'Sendero', meaning 'footpath'; ❷; **45min**) turn right, up the **Camino de la Cuesta del Cielo**. *(The Short and Alternative walks carry straight on here.)* The *camino* winds up to a crest. After about five minutes, there are a few waymarked short-cuts which avoid the bends and make for a steeper, but far more pleasant, climb. The views become ever more spectacular as you make your way to the CREST (**1h24min**).

As you begin to descend, a little cluster of cottages is just about visible through a gap ahead. Cross the bed of the **Arroyo del Romero** and, a little further on, reach a CONCRETE STORAGE SHED on the right (❸; **1h30min**). You will turn off here later but, if you wish to save almost an hour, skip to the 2h27min-point of the walk. Otherwise continue uphill, eventually reaching the cottages — the **Cortijos de la Civila** (❹; **2h02min**), said to be named after a woman occupant who used to dress as a Civil Guard. Just beyond the last cottage are the ruins of an old bread oven and an *era*. Amongst the prickly pears and the wildflowers, the land is still worked, and the almond trees produce a good harvest. It is a delightful spot and worth the climb. Mountaineers camp here before tackling the ascent of Ciclo and the peaks beyond. (The path to Cielo, with its fabulous views, is very well waymarked; it takes a little over 3h up and back down to the *cortijos*.)

Retrace your steps to the SHED (❸; **2h27min**); it has been built straight across the path you must now take. So make your way round behind it, to where the path is still clear. It descends a bit, then climbs diagonally across the hillside to the brow, from where there are views to Maro and the sea. Your next objective, the Cortijo Molinero, can be seen on the hill ahead. Descend again, through rosemary, gorse and a pine wood. Climb alongside an open area with remnants of hunters' fires, to the roofless ruin, the **Cortijo Molinero** (❺; **2h48min**). This spot is a must for a break. From the other side of the *cortijo* there are far-reaching views down the Sanguino Valley to Maro and Nerja, while the mountains of the Sierra de Almijara and Sierra de Tejeda lie to the west. Perched on rocks up here in the sunshine, we felt close to the gods as we watched first a booted eagle then four short-toed eagles rise from the valley and soar above us. What a sight!

Retrace your steps from the *cortijo* and, after about 50m, take the path which forks off to the right — close to a tall thick pine tree that stands alone. The path winds down gradually, obscured in places by the bushes overgrowing the sides, but always clear. Look out for, and take care not to miss, your next turn (❻; **3h06min**) on a clearly WAYMARKED PATH going off to the right. It descends quite steeply, and the vegetation on either side encroaches significantly. The path runs high above the Sanguino Valley, occasionally zigzagging to ease the descent. It takes you down to where a rocky *barranco* crosses your way (**3h27min**).

This is the bed of the **Arroyo Sanguino** (❼)**,** a continuation of the **Arroyo del Romero**. Turn left

and settle down to a long walk, negotiating the stones, rocks and large boulders in the shady river bed. Take advantage of the paths which sometimes take you out of the bed and along the banks. The valley opens out for a short while, with an olive grove on the right, then a CAVE on the left (**4h14min**). Giant reeds and lavender grow profusely along this part of the route (this is where your long trousers will be needed), and then the path takes you along the edge of an olive grove. Your way becomes a track passing

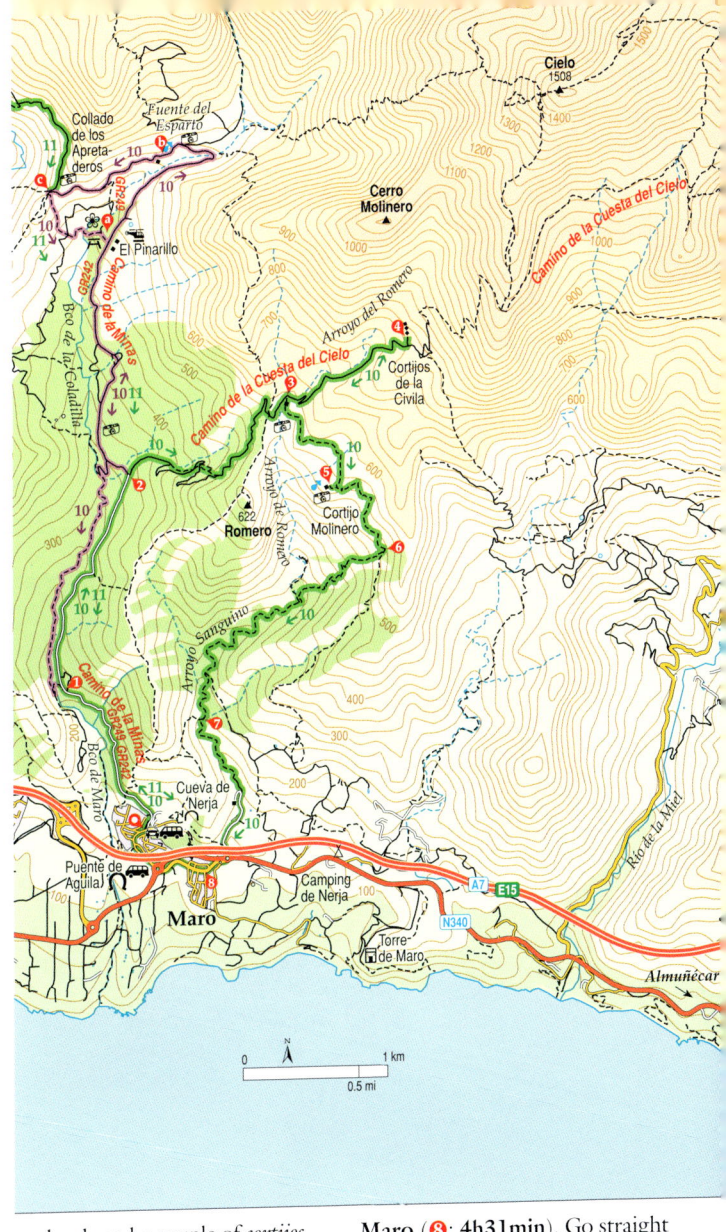

orchards and a couple of *cortijos* before going through a TUNNEL UNDER THE MOTORWAY. Take the second exit from the first roundabout (on the Maro bypass) and the first exit from the next roundabout. This brings you to main street on the north side of Maro (**8**; **4h31min**). Go straight over the roundabout just beyond the village, walk under the motorway again and then up to the CAR PARK at the **Cueva de Nerja** (**4h46min**).

89

Walk 11: CAMI DE LAS CABRAS (IBEX TRAIL)

See map pages 88-89; see also photo on page 29
Distance: 14km/8.7mi; 5h
Grade: 🔴 moderate, with some steep ascents/descents of 780m/2560ft overall. Easy navigation, clear paths and tracks throughout. Two river crossings which will be difficult after heavy rains. The area is remote, so make sure you are prepared.
Equipment: see page 51; trekking pole(s), towel and extra socks recommended; *walking boots are essential.*

How to get there: 🚌 to Nerja and on to Frigiliana (Timetables 3a, 5). Return 🚌 from La Cueva de Nerja (Timetables 3a, 3b).
Short walk: La Molineta (3.6km/2.3mi; 1h). 🔵 Easy; all on surfaced road or track; equipment as page 51; access as main walk. Follow the *Alternative walk* to ⓘ. Explore this delightful little hamlet and return (steeply!) the same way.
Alternative walk: Frigiliana, rivers circuit (9.3km/5.8mi; 3h). 🔴 Moderate, with ascents/descents of 320m/1050ft overall, some

La Molineta (Alternative walk and Short walk 2)

Walk 11: Camí de las Cabras

sections steep. Unless there has been a good spell of dry weather, this walk will involve wading, at least ankle deep, across fords and down the fast-flowing river. (The walk could be done from **Nerja** beach by walking up the track alongside the Río Chillar and picking up the walk at the river junction at **f** (the 1h12min-point); allow about *1h40min extra* out and back.) Equipment and access as main walk. **Start** from the main square in **Frigiliana** (**O**). Take the lane between Restaurante/Bar Virtudes and the Unicaja, signposted to the tourist office (Cuesta del Apero). Follow this main street all the way to where the bypass road comes in from the right at a roundabout. Keep on the bypass to just before ehe entrance to house No 7, then go left on a concrete walkway (18min). Follow this steeply downhill into the little hamlet of **La Molineta** (24min). Go straight on, passing the **Molino de Aceite** (**d**) off to the right. Descend steeply on a concrete track and wind down to the **Río Higuerón** (**e**; 30min). Turn right, downstream, and walk (or wade) along the pebbly river bed. At the junction with the wide bed of the **Río Chillar** (just before the motorway; **f**; 1h12min), turn left on a track and follow it upstream to a lane on the far side and turn left. At a QUARRY (**g**; 1h20min) walk over to the large isolated eucalyptus tree. From here a track, initially concreted, re-crosses the river and takes you steeply up the opposite bank to the ridge above. Pass some villas and turn right at a T-junction (1h40min). At the Y-junction 160m further on, fork right, up towards a pylon and a small peak. You pass several villas on this lane. At a junction where four tracks fan out ahead of you (**h**; 1h52min), take the third from the left, passing to the right of a house, and head uphill. A few PR waymarks begin to appear now, as you continue up into the hills, for a while out of sight of all habitation. Frigiliana comes into view, and for a short time you head away from it. The track becomes a narrow rocky path, crosses a dip and reaches the ruins of a *cortijo* (**i**; 2h29min). A narrow path then takes you directly towards Frigiliana and descends to the fast-flowing **Río Higuerón**. Turn right, upstream, cross over at a POST, and follow a steep concrete track up to **Frigiliana** (3h).

Development in and around Frigiliana means that it is not the charming little whitewashed village that it used to be. However, it still provides the tourist with a good day out and the walker with the starting point for this fantastic hike (part of the waymarked GR249, the 'Malaga Trail'. As close to a wilderness experience as can be found so close to the coast, this walk cannot fail to impress. Views and scenery are almost too amazing and all-encompassing to put into words — you *must* experience them for yourself. There is always water in the Río Chillar and, unless there has been a long spell of dry weather, be prepared to get your feet wet as you cross it halfway through the walk. Ignore any red *dots* you may see; just follow the red/white GR249/242 all the way.

Start from the main square in **Frigiliana**, the Plaza del Ingenio (⬤). Take the *downhill* lane between Restaurante/Bar Virtudes and the Unicaja, with signposts on the left for Río Higuerón and the GR242. This becomes a concrete track and descends steeply to the bed of the Río Higuerón, named for a fig tree (*higuera*) which once grew near its source. The concrete track bends sharp left by a pylon, opposite a large cave. About 150m past here the concrete runs out, and you are on a very stony track in the bed of the **Río Higuerón**. In winter, a quite spectacular waterfall can be seen up to the left — where there is also an *acequia*. This *acequia* and the track you are on converge at the **Pozo Batán**, a reservoir used to regulate the water in the channel. It used to be a popular swimming hole, but is now fenced off. About 100m further on, leave the river bed to the right (❶; **18min**) and head uphill on a narrow path. There is only a sign here 'Zona de Reserva' in red letters, but it is closely followed by a red/white GR waymarked post.

After climbing steadily and steeply through pines, you reach a

Molino de Aciete in La Molineta; left: Frigiliana

RIDGE (**44min**) from where the summit of Cielo stands out prominently ahead to the left. The GR traverses the ridge, the slopes either side resplendent with gorse, rosemary and, in spring, wildflowers in bloom. At a faint Y-FORK (**51min**), follow the GR to the right, down off the ridge (not waymarked, but there is a sign, 'Propriedad Privada' off to the left. The path heads right, hugging the slopes, and eventually takes you to a CREST (**1h07min**), from where the pointed peak of Navachica dominates the view.

The path undulates across the slopes, now pine-covered. Notice a LIME KILN on the left (**❷**; **1h14min**) and, as the path bends sharp right (**1h24min**), go up, then down, between large rocks. There soon follows a steep climb (**1h39min**) as the path zigzags up a rocky gully. You might be lucky, as we were once, to be greeted at the top by a *cabra montés*.

Now you begin the DESCENT TO THE RÍO CHILLAR (**❸**; **1h49min**). Take care — you'll be grateful for your trekking pole in places. As you descend, notice your onward path on the opposite side of the valley. At a WAYMARKING POST just before reaching the river, a path goes left upstream to a reservoir (a lovely picnic spot), but you turn right and reach the **Río Chillar** (**❹**; **2h14min**). You pass a few inviting picnic areas on the banks of the river: take advantage of them (unless you're going to the reservoir), then cross at the ford.

You reach a WAYMARKING POST on the opposite bank at the start of a stony path, eroded in places. Zigzag up, crossing an *acequia* (**❺**; **2h40min**; it also leads to the reservoir, but is a bit vertiginous).

Reaching a track at another WAYMARKING POST (**3h09min**), look across to Frigiliana and the rugged terrain you have negotiated so far — it's impressive!

A left turn on this track also leads to the reservoir, but the main walk turns right, to a major junction at a saddle, the **Collado de los Apretaderos** (**C**; **3h21min**). A WAYMARKING POST points left here, at the point where Alternative walk 10 comes in from the Fuente del Esparto. But you should walk a few metres towards the two paths which rise up to the right. Your onward, descending, path is just before them, marked by a POST WITH A WHITE ARRROW on the left; it is narrow and indistinct at first.

From here follow the notes for *Alternative walk 10* from the 1h48min-point (page 86). To avoid a stretch of track walking, fork right about 25 minutes from **El Pinarillo** and follow *Short walk 10* (page 85) in the **Barranco de la Coladilla** — from just before **❷** (the 52min-point) until it climbs back to the track. Continue on the track to **La Cueva de Nerja** (**5h**).

Walk 12: FABRICA DE LA LUZ AND PUERTO BLANQUILLO

Distance: 10km/6.2mi; 4h30min (or 11.8km/7.3mi; 4h10min if returning by unmade road)
Grade: ● moderate, with ascent/descent of 550m/1800ft
Equipment: see page 51; trekking pole(s) useful
How to get there and return: 🚗 to Santa Ana in Canillas de Albaida (the 42km-point of Car tour 3), then continue to the right (signed to 'La Fábrica'). Pass a quarry and, 1km futher on, park at the *fábrica* (36° 51.818'N, 3°58.218'W).
Short walk: *Cueva del Melero* (2.6km/1.6mi; 50min; ● Easy. Just walk to the Cortijo del Chato (❶), from where you can see the enormous cave and return the same way.

This walk is all about the charm of a rural river valley, with a bounding stream at the start and passages along herb-clad hillsides. The *fábrica*, an old hydroelectric plant and now an attractive *zona recreativa*, is a particularly popular spot on Sundays and *fiestas*. On a weekday, when it is likely to be deserted, its peace and tranquillity are almost tangible.

Start at the *fábrica* (○; *P*12) by crossing the LOG BRIDGE just below the toilet block and head upstream on a charming little path alongside the **Arroyo de la Cueva de Melero**. Cross the stream on STEPPING STONES (**6min**), the first of several such crossings. After rain be prepared to get your feet wet. Always accompanied by the sound of flowing water and waterfalls low and high, you climb gradually, the path now quite rocky.

You arrive at the **Cortijo del Chato** (❶; **25min**), its fruit groves stretched out either side of your path. The huge mouth of the **Cueva de Melero** opens up on a hillside to the left. You move away from the riverside here and pick up an unsurfaced road which you follow upstream for over 700m. Then, at the right of a small dam (probably dry), the track fizzles out and you move to the *arroyo* again, on a footpath. The water in the river bed now disappears; it flows under gravel now almost all the way to the saddle where you are aiming — unless it has been a particularly rainy year.

The path steepens, and you should head left on a track (❷) and then go right on a path below the **Cortijo de Chaparral** (❸; **50min**) — the buildings are above, in a side valley, almost hidden among eucalyptus and pines. When you pass these terraces, you come upon the **Barranco de la Mina**, with a usually permanent flow of water.

Ten-15 minutes further on you are below another *cortijo* in ruins — the **Cortijo Camacho** (❹). Be sure to close any gates here, to avoid livestock escaping —

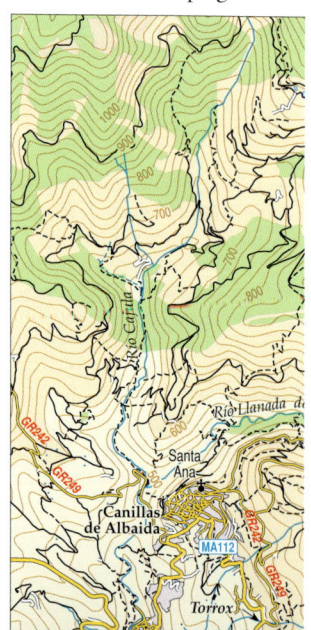

At the Fábrica de la Luz zona recreativa

livestock farming still goes on here.

Then, moving through dense bush, you cross the **Barranco de la Fuente de la Teja**, another permanent stream. After this crossing and a final steep climb, you arrive at a 'motorway' — the wide motorable track from Canillas de Albaida (**5**). A CAIRN indicates a left turn, and you reach the **Puerto Blanquillo** (**6**; **2h30min**), a fine *mirador*.

Unless you have arranged for someone to meet you here, you *could* take the 'motorway' back almost to your starting point. If you take the track, you will pass a *fuente* on the left. Some 1km further on, 100m past a firebreak, where a track crosses, take the downhill *path* on the right between marker stones. But in truth it's preferable to just retrace your steps…

Once back at the **Fábrica de la Luz** (**4h10min-4h30min**), have a well-deserved rest beside the surging waters.

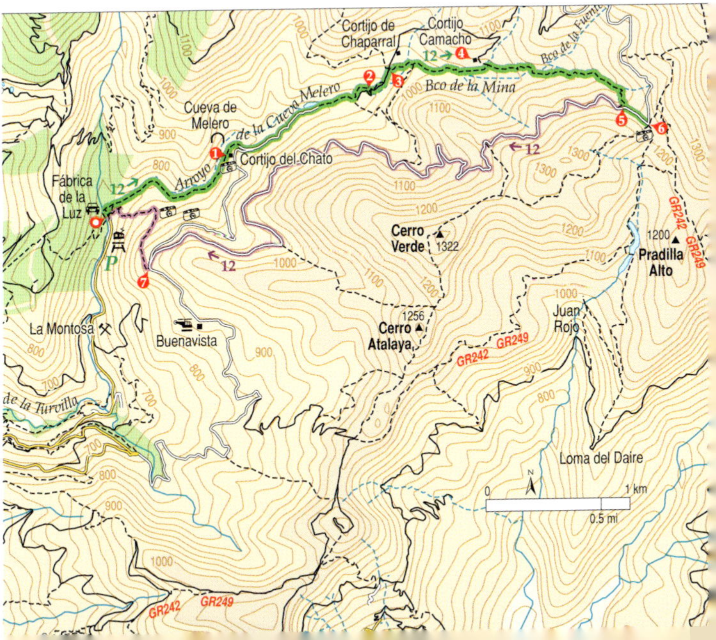

Walk 13: ALCAUCIN VALLEY: VENTAS DE ZAFARRAYA TO PUENTE DON MANUEL

Distance: 12.1km/7.5mi; 3h51min
Grade: 🔵-🔴 easy-moderate, with a descent of 700m/2295ft
Equipment: see page 51.
How to get there and return: 🚌 to/from Puente Don Manuel (also known as Puente de Salia; the 83km-point on Car tour 3); park in the shade under the eucalyptus trees at the junction by the Ermita del Puente de Don Manuel (36° 54.978'N, 4°7.690'W). Then walk towards the A402; your bus stop is just before you get there, on the right, opposite the Restaurante La Era. Take the bus to Ventas de Zafarraya (Timetable 6); alight in the centre of Ventas de Zafarraya, close to the church.

Alternative walk: Sleepy hamlets (9.5km/5.9mi; 3h50min). This will suit those who can't make the early bus or who prefer a circular walk. 🔴 Moderate, with ascent/descent of about 320m/1050ft. Access: drive to Puente Don Manuel (as above), then continue north on the A402 for about another 4.3km. Keep an eye out for a road on the right with a red and wide yellow banding on a 'Stop' sign. Turn right here (*not signposted* when last seen). After 400m, at a junction, park where you can, courteously; you will see the *boquete* ahead. Walk north along the road (signed to LAS HUERTAS); it's the very narrow and quiet Camino Real de Granada. In just a few minutes it forks left and starts to climb steadily. Continue on, ignoring all turn offs. It's steep in a few places, but you can pause and take time to look around you. There's a wonderful view of the Boquete de Zafarraya (30min) and the tiny hamlets you pass through seem remnants of a bygone age. After 3km, turn sharp right on another lane at a CROSSROADS AT HOUSES (1h14min) and carry on to **Espino** (❷; 1h36min). To the left you'll see the *fuente* where you pick up the main walk at the 44min-point. Follow it back to your car at the crossroads (3h50min).

This walk is not only a birders' delight, but has the added attraction of being almost all downhill! It takes you through countryside where life is lived much as it used to be hundreds of years ago. Don't be surprised to meet old men on donkeys, oxen and horses ploughing in the fields, goats being taken for a walk on leads, or flocks of sheep obstructing the pathways. In spring you'll encounter men high in the branches of olive trees beating the fruit off with sticks, while the women below gather it up into buckets and baskets. You will encounter some noisy dogs en route, but they are either chained, or friendly and timid.

The bus journey up from Puente Don Manuel is an experience in itself. The road winds higher and higher, until you feel as if you are on top of the world. The Boquete de Zafarraya, a huge U-shaped pass between rocky cliffs, looms ever closer as the altitude increases. Just beyond the pass, where the palms and fruit trees of the lower altitudes are left behind, look on the right, and you'll see the path this walk

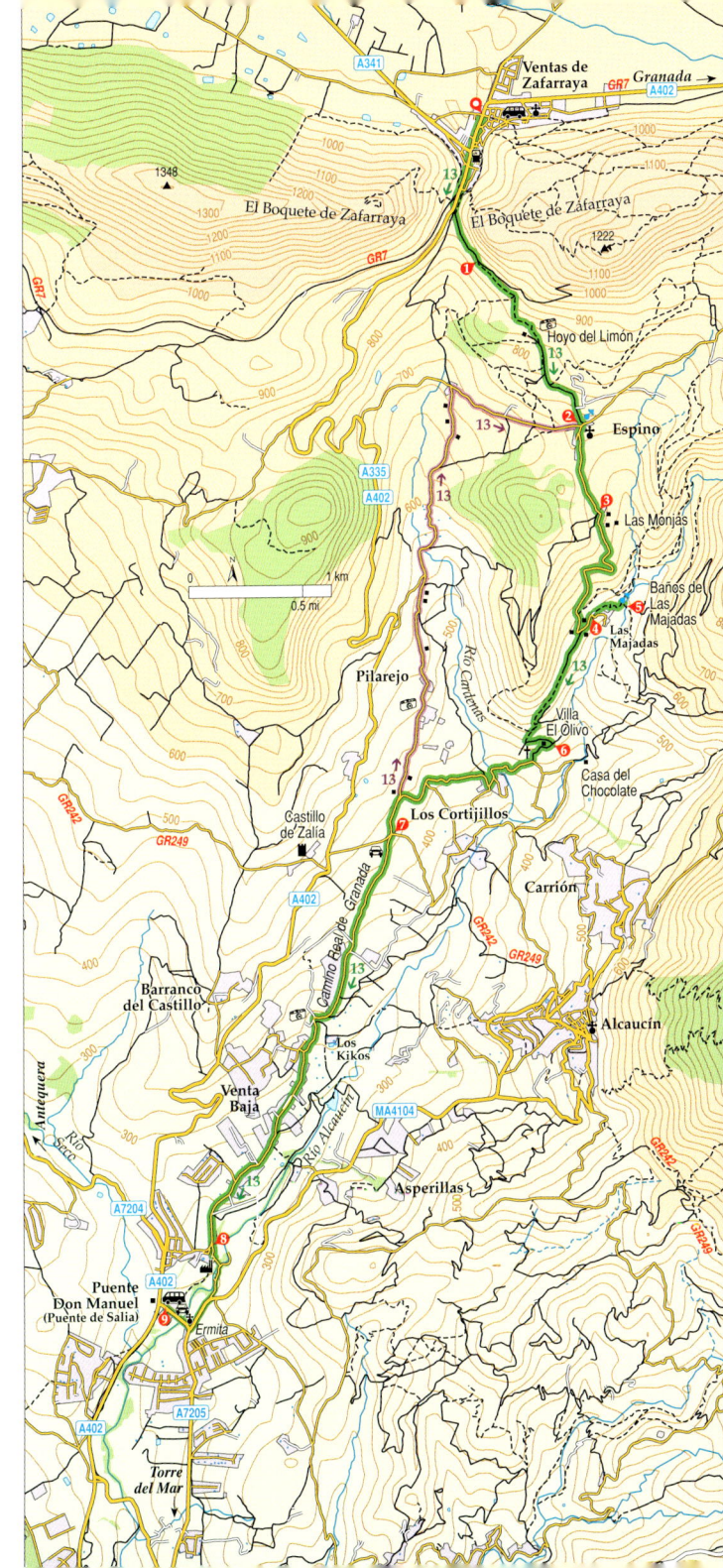

follows close to the road. You may find it a bit chilly in the early morning mists up on this high plateau, but the sun will soon find you as you descend.

Take a moment to look at the interesting fountain in the church square in **Ventas de Zafarraya** before setting off. Then **start the walk** (⭕): leave the village the way the bus brought you in. Pass the PETROL STATION and *pensión* and go under the BRIDGE. This bridge used to carry the rack-railway line to Vélez-Málaga; it was dismantled in the 1960s, but parts of the line still mark the boundary between the provinces of Granada and Málaga. Almost immediately, go off the road to the left, taking the narrow stony PATH which runs alongside the road.

After just a few metres fork left again on a track. Ignore the chain and the 'Peligro' (Danger) sign; it only applies to vehicles. The track soon veers away from the road and skirts round the foot of tall cliffs, home to choughs and ravens. Nearer ground level, the rocks are alive with small birds including black wheatear and rock bunting. Look down on the Río Alcaucín and the mountain ranges that stretch far into the distance beyond the Embalse de Viñuela. And cast a glance back occasionally at the remarkable sight of the Boquete de Zafarraya.

Fuente *at Espino, with El Boquete de Zafarraya behind it. The* fuente *looks very different now, with a curved, crazy-paved backing, but the view to the Boquete de Zafarraya is the same!*

Be sure not to miss your fork to the right (**❶**; **25min**), where the track continues up the mountain. Your path leaves the cliffs behind and descends through open countryside. Sage and gorse add a brilliant splash of colour to the landscape in springtime. It's not long before the village of Espino comes into sight, overlooked by the Sierra de Tejeda, a range dominated by the huge barren mass of Maroma. This is a glorious part of the walk. Mountains surround you in every direction, and the air is filled with the sound of stonechats and larks (wood, thekla and sky). Bird song mingles with the sound of goat and sheep bells, as you cross an expanse of grassland (**34min**) and pass a little almond grove, well tended despite its apparent isolation.

When the path becomes a grassy track, notice the old walls of an *era* over on the left. Wind down between cultivated terraces and enter **Espino** at the *fuente* shown left (**❷**; **44min**). *(The Alternative walk comes in here from the right.)* Pass the church and immediately fork left on a narrow concreted track which descends past a line of cypress trees to the fields. From a collection of houses called **Las Monjas** (**❸**; **54min**) continue downhill. You soon spot the houses of Las Majadas below, and the larger village of Alcaucín in the distance. The track turns sharply left downhill (**1h13min**) towards Las Majadas. Follow it, but notice a track going back off to the right — your ongoing route. In **Las Majadas** (**❹**; **1h20min**) you pass a small orange grove and go down between the houses of this charmingly tiny hamlet. At the bottom, beyond an orchard, make for a tall ELECTRICITY POST and from there take a narrow path down left to the river. (The path is in bad condition and a bit tricky, but just make your way down through the oleanders as best you can.) The sound of the water will lead you to an old sulphur spring and pools, the **Baños de Las Majadas** (**❺**; **1h35min**), used since the times of the Moors.

Retrace your steps back to the houses and then up to the track mentioned earlier (**1h52min**), and head off left at the bend. This old trail, which used to serve the hamlets below, is now used by hunters and shortly becomes a path which rises above an olive grove. On the opposite side of the deep gorge you'll see an *acequia* and perhaps a line of beehives close to the Casa del Chocolate.

The rocky path contours high above the cultivated valley, heading directly towards the shimmering waters of the Embalse de Viñuela in the far distance. Lined with rosemary and violets, the path then descends gently along the top of another olive grove. At the end of this grove, the path becomes indistinct. Follow it as it drops down the edge of the grove — onto a stony track, where you turn left. The track brings you out onto a narrow asphalt road with a RENTAL VILLA just to the right (Villa El Olivo; ❻; **2h30min**).

Turn right, pass the villa and a decorative SHRINE on the right, and settle down to enjoy the remainder of the walk which will take you along quiet country lanes, past several houses and *cortijos,* and through olive groves and rural villages. Preoccupied with the sights and sounds of the countryside, you'll soon forget the asphalt beneath your feet. Cross a stream, the **Río Cárdenas**, a lovely spot when the water flows strongly, and begin to climb a little, just for a change. As a road comes in from the right, your road levels out again, and fig trees begin to appear among the olive trees. You are now walking on the medieval **Camino Real de Granada** which runs all the way to Puente Don Manuel. Cross a dip and go straight ahead at a CROSSROADS — where another backward look at the Boquete is called for. *(The Alternative walk starts and finishes here.)* Descending again, olives give way to citrus fruits, pomegranates and apricots.

Pass between the few houses of **Los Kikos** (**3h20min**) and look over to the right for the ruins of the Castillo de Zalía perched on a hill. Founded by the Phoenicians and reconstructed by the Arabs, little remains of it today.

At the far end of the longer village of **Venta Baja** (**3h39min**), FORK LEFT DOWNHILL (❽), past a workshop and round below an olive oil FACTORY with a tall chimney. (There used to be a little notice at this fork announcing that you are on the ancient route of Ibn Batûta, the 14th-century voyager from Tangiers, who journeyed through southern Spain from Málaga to Granada.)

The lane takes you between giant eucalyptus trees, across the river and past the factory's residue pools. A little further on it brings you to a wider road: turn right and follow it to your car at the **Puente Don Manuel** junction by the *ermita* (**3h51min**), a few metres short of the bus stop at ❾, where you can refresh yourself at one of the many bar/restaurants.

Walk 14: THREE WALKS IN EL CHORRO NATURAL PARK

See also cover photo
a Sendero del Gaitanejo and Mirador de los Embalses (5.4km/3.3mi; 1h40min). ● Easy, with a descent/ascent of about 200m/650ft. 🚌 to the 113.5km-point of Car tour 4. (Approaching from Ardales, turn right on a narrow road just before the tunnel.) Park just above the Restaurante El Mirador (36° 55.729'N, 4°48.061'W). Equipment as page 51 (but trainers will suffice). See description overleaf.

b Mirador de los Buitreras (9.3km/5.8mi; 3h). ● Strenuous; ascents/descents of 500m/1640ft. Access as Walk a; equipment as on page 51. Description overleaf.

c Caminito del Rey from the Visitors' Centre (6.5km/4mi; 3h). ●❗❗ Strenuous, with constant ups and downs of about 500m/1640ft, mostly on steps (some narrow and ladder-like). You must be very fit and agile. *Danger of vertigo!* To get there park at the Visitors' Centre at the junction of the MA9006 and MA5403 (36° 54.889'N, 4°48.406'W). Equipment as on page 51, plus hard hat which you will be given. Before attempting this walk, *it is imperative* that you visit www.caminitodelrey.info to register, read the rules and buy a ticket. But *do* look at a video first (see Walk c, page 102-3). The walk is closed Mon, also Dec 24, 25 and Jan 31.

See this! Whether you are an adventurous walker or heights trouble you, the El Chorro Natural Park has to be seen. There is so much to do in glorious surroundings. While some landscapers will find the 'jewel' of the site (Walk c) too vertiginous, we suggest two alternatives; Walk a incorporates a path along the side of the lake — a delight for botanists and birdwatchers, while Walk b takes you to vulture territory. Plan to spend at least a day, walking, picnicking or even swimming in one of the reservoirs in Malaga's 'Lake District'.

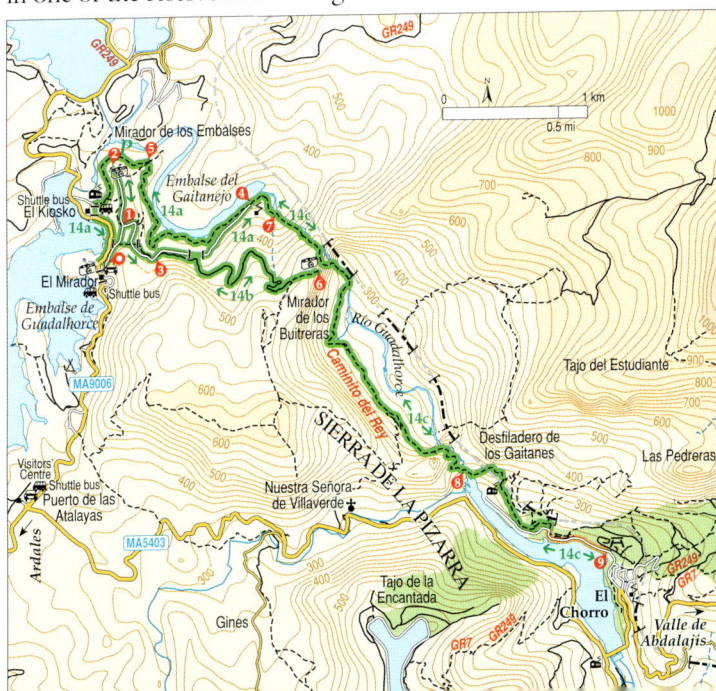

102   Landscapes of Andalucía

Walk a: Start out at the CAR PARK above the Mirador restaurant (⓪): walk up the road, past its *mirador*, to a junction with the Sendero del Gaitanejo (❶; **5min**). Later you'll take the right fork but, for now, turn left for a 15-minute return trip to the more revealing **Mirador de los Embalses** (❷; **13min**; *P*14). From its platform there is a splendid panorama over the reservoirs of the Lakes District, while on the other side of the viewpoint, the grandeur of the gorge is visible from the cliff-top (*P*14). Then return to the junction (❶; **20min**) and turn left on a track, through the yellow barrier. It's all downhill to the river from here. At a junction (❸; **26min**), continue straight along the track to the left. *(Walk b turns right here.)*

As you gradually descend, look for tits, buntings, finches, redstarts and warblers, and, at the right time of year, enjoy the variety of wildflowers. Beyond a short TUNNEL (**33min**), look back at the network of caves around it. The track ends at an ELECTRICITY SUBSTATION (❹; **39min**), the entrance to the **Caminito del Rey**. Before it is a VISITORS' RECEPTION (where those doing *the* walk are handed a hard hat which must be worn throughout).

Turn sharp left here; continue on a track bordering the edge of the **Embalse del Gaitanejo** (**51min**). Eucalypts and conifers provide ample shade as you wander along, possibly disturbing one of the grey herons which fish from the banks of the river.

The track eventually rises round some marshy areas and passes along the foot of a cliff where caves have, in the past, provided shelter for animals. It becomes a path and snakes steadily up to a SADDLE (❺; **1h16min**). Turn left on the main path, ignoring a narrow path which forks up left (this leads up to the Mirador de los Embalses in three or four minutes). Your path descends briefly before settling down to contour around the slopes. Meet a dirt road and turn left through another short TUNNEL (**1h28min**). This brings you to the main road, where restaurants overlook the reservoir. Turn left and, about six or seven minutes later (at the end of the crash barrier and just before a TUNNEL), go up the bank to the left on an indistinct path which leads to the *mirador* close to your car above the RESTAURANT (**1h40min**).

Walk b: Follow Walk a to ❸, then take the track on the *right*, for a fairly strenuous 'out and back'. The rocky track rises, then levels out, before climbing steadily towards overhead cables. It's a steep climb, but the encircling views provide ample excuse for frequent pauses. Within about 20 minutes a long zigzag takes you to a short level stretch, from where the El Chorro gorge is clearly visible. After a further 12-13 minutes of zig-zagging upwards, the track peters out. Continue straight ahead along a narrow and

The walk in the natural park is without doubt the Caminito del Rey. This photo shows the narrow walkway, the boardwalks and some of the steps. You can see how the new boardwalks (totalling 3km), were built above the old concrete paths (without railings!). This photo also shows how far above the Río Guadalhorce the path runs and the almost transparent protection at the side; what it does not *show in this calm stretch, is the sensation one feels when the river is surging and roaring below in the Desfiladero de los Gaitanes, where the gorge is at its most narrow; only those with no fear of heights can bear to look into the river.*

overgrown, but clear path. Within a few minutes you're at the **Mirador de Las Buitreras** (❻; **1h20min**) overlooking the whole of the **El Chorro Natural Park** — well worth the climb, especially when you are joined at the summit by vultures (*buitreras* means 'vultures'). Retrace your steps to ❸ and continue to follow Walk a, arriving back at the car park in **3h**.

Walk c: Before you log onto the caminodelrey.info website, please take a look at YouTube. There are several videos of this walk, but we would recommend the one by Steve Marsh, 'El Caminito del Rey: what it's *really* like to walk this path'. It's long enough to show you the awkward places (the ladder-like, narrow steps, the places where you might bang your head and knock yourself out …) and especially the potential for vertigo. Although there is a railing and a cable on the side of the walk with the drop, there is also a cable attached to the rock on the other side … and you will see many people holding on to both! As the photo on page 103 shows, the railing on the side above the gorge is purposely as transparent as possible, to give walkers the frisson of excitement.

History: This walkway was originally built between 1901 and 1905 to allow workmen to access an *acqueia* carryig water from one of the reservoirs down to the hydroelectric plant at El Chorro, a drop of about 100m/330ft. The name, 'The King's Little Walkway' comes from the upgrading of the project with the Embalse de Guadalhorce, which King Alfonso XIII opened 1921. The *caminito* runs more or less parallel with this *acequia,* but it is mostly in tunnels. You see it when you cross the bridge about halfway through the walk, where it is carried in an arched covered aquaduct beside the new path. To build the original *camino,* the workmen (many from the navy or prisons) were suspended from above by ropes. After several deaths among the daredevil walkers who braved the narrow path, it was closed in the 1990s. But it was rebuilt in one year in 2014 and opened in 2015. There is a video about the construction of the new walkway on YouTube called 'Así se hizo El Caminito del Rey'.

We haven't even tried to write up the walk, and have just put a couple of waypoints on the map and the GPS track — because you won't be looking at any guide or smartphone (except to take photos)! We urge you to watch the video mentioned above, and then, if you can 'stomach' the walk, buy your ticket at www.caminodelrey.info. We've given the distance and time to allow if you park at the Vistors' Centre on the MA9006 and take the shuttlebus to the start at the El Kiosko restaurant and are collected from the finish of the walk at El Chorro. But you do not *have* to do this; you could buy a ticket and make your own way to the *north* entrance ❹ — perhaps follow Walk a there. What is important is that you *must have a ticket and must start at the north entrance* (❹). If you come by shuttle bus and it disgorges its usual complement, you'll find yourself in a knot of walkers to begin, but they soon thin out and you can walk at your own pace.

Although the walkway is open all the time during daylight hours, we'd advise going in the morning to avoid the worst heat of the day.

Walk 15: RUTA CRUZ DE LA MISION

See photo on pages 36-37
Distance: 6.2km/3.8mi; 2h24min
Grade: ● easy-moderate, with an ascent/descent of about 240/787ft overall (the only sustained climbing being near the start). Well signposted and waymarked, sometimes with red dots.
Note that we have marked trail colours on the map to aid identification.
Equipment: see page 51.
How to get there and return:
🚐 to/from Mijas (Timetable 7); alight at the terminus in the main square. Or 🚗 to/from Mijas (the 17km-point on Car tour 5); park in the public car park below the town hall (*Ayuntamiento*) and go up steps to the main square.

Short walk: Ermita del Calvario and Cantera del Barrio (3km/2mi; 1h03min). ● Easy, but it is a short stiff climb of about 120m/395ft to the *ermita*. Access and equipment as main walk, but trainers will suffice. Follow the main walk to ❻ (40min), then continue on the track as it bends left and continues below a quarry.

At 49min, on a hairpin bend close to a green water building, ignore the steep path which descends directly to the road. Instead, follow the track to the road (55min) and turn left. Pass the *mirador* and, just before the Camino del Calvario, turn right and make your way down into the village (1h03min).

Alternative walk: Blue and yellow trails (4.3km/2.7mi; 1h12min). ● Moderate, with an ascent/descent of 370m/1215ft. Follow the main walk to the 24min-point at ❸ and turn right on a path marked with BLUE DOTS. Climb fairly steeply to reach a LEVEL SECTION (**35min**) — a suitable spot to catch your breath and survey the extensive views over Mijas. At a JUNCTION just a few minutes later (❾; **38min**), where the 'blue' path continues upwards to the ridge and the Málaga peak (gaining about another 200m of altitude), you take the signposted 'yellow' route to the right. It has some YELLOW WAYMARKS and zigzags down to a point east of the *ermita* (**1h**). Retrace your outward route back into **Mijas** (**1h12min**).

Situated close to the coast with an impressive mountain backdrop, Mijas provides the day-trip tourist with a plethora of souvenir shops, restaurants, bars and *burro*-taxis. Nevertheless, as you make your way up to the Ermita del Calvario, you will realise that it has managed to retain much of the charm of a typical Andalusian village. The remainder of the walk takes you across the slopes of the Sierra de Mijas, where the variety of trees and vegetation is guaranteed to excite the botanist and delight any nature lover. These southern slopes are prone to wildfires, and many of the pines have still not recovered. But views over Mijas and the coast have opened out, and the ravaged land has regenerated with lavender, rosemary, gorse and a plethora of wildflowers. You'll see various coloured waymarks as you walk — *ignore all but those we specifically mention*. The Mijas tourist board has issued a map showing all the waymarked walks in the sierra; it's available online: www.turimo.mijas.es>nature>trekking.

Start out from the grand white TOWN HALL in **Mijas** (**O**), just opposite the bus terminus. With your back to its clock, cross the road, turn left and go around the block into a wooded square. Pass souvenir shops and restaurants and leave the square at the corner, through Pasaje Salvador Cantos Jimenez, signposted to the Centro Histórico. Go up steps and into **Plaza de la Libertad**. Almost immediately take the slope, the pretty Calle San Sebastian, up to the right, past the front of a church. As it becomes Calle La Cruz, you will see the words 'Camino del Calvario' etched into the pathway. This is the start of the pilgrimage trail which takes you past the 14 Stations of the Cross. With the expansion of the village, only a few still remain. From here keep zigzagging up steps. Just below a pylon, turn right and go up steps to the main road, the A387, which runs along the top of the village.

Cross the road and take the initially concreted path with wooden railings which starts 30 metres to the right (**❶**; **6min**). There are info boards and signposts with RED/WHITE/YELLOW WAYMARKS at the top of the railed section, and you can just see the *ermita* above. The path — which is also the GR249 — will zigzag steeply up to it, through pine trees and past some remaining crosses. At CROSS VIII, make sure you follow the main path sharp left (signed and waymarked), ignoring the path straight ahead (the return route for the Alternative walk). From the **Ermita del Calvario** (**❷**; **16min**; *P*15; photo on pages 36-37), you look down over Mijas, encircled by its impressive sierra, and will see just how high you have climbed. Pause for a moment to pick out the village bullring and amphitheatre.

Pass in front of the *ermita* and continue on the path which cuts diagonally up the slope. As the woods thicken, the path steepens. At a SIGNPOSTED JUNCTION (**❸**; **24min**) keep straight ahead, following red dots. *(The Alternative walk turns right here, following blue dots.)* Further on, look upwards to see the little whitewashed dome for which this trail is named — the **Cruz de la Misión**, atop a mound (**❹**; **28min**).

The path soon leads to the upper level of the disused **Cantera del Barrio** (**❺**; **31min**), a marble quarry, with an ABANDONED BUILDING (originally intended as a walkers' hostel) and a small NURSERY below. Follow the path

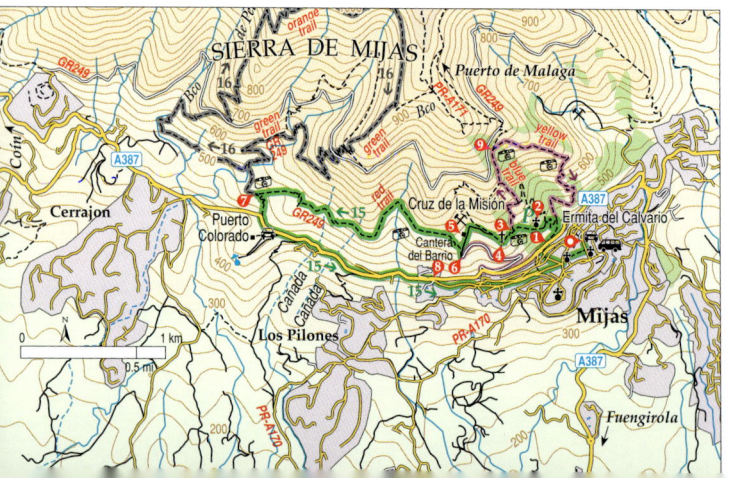

Walk 15: Ruta Cruz de la Misión 107

across the quarry, past the building, where chunks of marble still lie about.

As the track you are on curves left downhill, turn sharp right on a NARROW PATH lined with herbs and lavender (**6**; **40min**). *(But for the Short walk, continue on the track back to the main road.)* The path (with RED/WHITE GR WAYMARKING POSTS) takes you steeply up the left-hand edge of the quarry. It continues rising quite steeply, cutting diagonally left, with fine views all the way down to the coast. Soon (**45min**) you'll descend for a little while, then the path undulates, always hugging the hillside and mostly shored up by rocks which create a narrow terrace. Signposting and waymarking is excellent.

Eventually (**56min**) you cross an old stabilised small rocky landslip and go round a *cañada*. As the terracing disappears and the slope levels out on the left, the path becomes less stony. The terracing now comes and goes, and a short break in the trees (**1h15min**) reveals the valley of the Río Fuengirola and hills rolling into the formidable Sierra Blanca (not to be confused with the other Sierra Blanca to the west of Marbella).

Descend to cross another *cañada* (**1h23min**) and be prepared for a complete and unexpected change in vegetation. This north-facing slope supports a forest of eucalyptus trees. The path, now narrower, may be somewhat overgrown and damp underfoot. After autumn rains you should see a variety of colourful mushrooms, some poisonous. The small ones tend to grow in clumps, while individuals of at least dinner-plate dimensions erupt through the soil like mini-volcanoes. Pines gradually begin to infiltrate the eucalyptus, and the path improves again.

A major JUNCTION (**7**; **1h40min**) is marked with several signposts. A sign points back to the way you've come on the red trail, and up to the right the green/orange and blue trails are indicated. Go straight on here and zigzag down through the trees (**1h46min**); this is an access trail from the main road for several walks, including Walk 16. On the far side of the road a huge water tank stands on top of a hill and, just below it, you'll see a small white building which used to serve as the village dog pound.

When you arrive on the road at the **Puerto Colorado**, turn left and walk along the verge, then cross to the pavement. You reach the outskirts of Mijas at a fork in the road (**8**; **2h05min**). Go right and walk straight through the old part of the village, between brilliantly white houses. Some of the streets off to the right have picturesque and interesting signs, like Plaza de los Siete Caños (Square of the Seven Spouts) and Callejo de los Gitanos (Gypsy Alley). Don't miss the little grottos on the left opposite number 85. It's a long village, but you eventually come to a fork at the **Cruz Roja** (Red Cross) building on the left. Head left uphill, to return to the TOWN HALL in **Mijas** (**2h24min**).

Walk 16: PICO MIJAS

See also photo on pages 36-37
Distance: 11km/6.8mi; 4-6h
Grade: 🟠-⚫ moderate-strenuous; ascents/descents of 700m/2295ft overall. There is no danger of vertigo, but *you must be agile* for negotiating the steep ascent and descent over rocky terrain. *Very little shade en route, start out early in the day and do not attempt in summer.*
Equipment: see page 51. There are no springs en route, so take extra water and also walking poles for the steep ascent/descent

How to get there and return: 🚗 Park at Puerto Colorado on the A387 a short way west of Mijas. This is a viewpoint/parking area opposite an info board and steps up to a access trail to several routes in the Mijas Sierra (36° 35.842'N, 4°39.725'W)
Alternative walks: You could start the walk by parking in Mijas Pueblo and visiting the Ermita del Calvario and Cruz de la Misión (as Walk 15). Then, for a really long walk, follow Walk 15 to ❼, then pick up Walk 16 at ❶.

This is the most popular of all the routes in the Sierra de Mijas, but it's not a walk in the park! It's best done on a clear winter's day; please do not attempt it in the summer heat. It can be in the 30°s C here even in winter, so we've not given any times for reaching certain points on this stiff climb — just take it gently at your own pace. And if you give up

Start this walk at **Puerto Colorado** (⭕) by crossing the A387 to the stepped path with wooden railings and an INFO BOARD. We are going to climb to the peak on the green trail (the Sendero de la Fuente de la Adelfa) and descend the orange route in the Barranco del Pedregal. This is an access link to several routes, so zigzag up through a light covering of pines to a JUNCTION (❶) where several routes are signposted. Walk 15 — the red route — comes in here from the right. All other routes head left; so go left and carry on to the next JUNCTION (❷), a narrow Y-fork where you go right (signed 'Cañada Fuente del la Aldefa'. Deeper zigzags now make the climbing less arduous, and already you have superb views down to the coast, all the better when the pines thin out.

At the next JUNCTION (❸), another Y-fork, go right. After a few metres of downhill walking, the trail hairpins uphill to the dusty, motorable FORESTRY TRACK. Follow it to the right a few paces, then continue on your UPWARD PATH (❹); a WAYMARKER POST WITH A GREEN SQUARE confirms your route, and the *bola* (ball) on the top of Pico Mijas is in full view — as are the antennas.

At the next junction you *leave* the green trail. Go left, following 'ENLACE SENDERO PICO MIJAS' (❺; Link Trail to Pico Mijas). It has no assigned colour: you may have wondered, when we said that you would climb on the green route to the peak when the green route is well to the east of it. Although narrow in places, this trail is in fine condition, but the pines have disappeared, replaced by low vegetation, and there's no shade. The trail, clear throughout,

Typical path on the Sierra de Mijas: often, you can seek shade, but basically the walks are open to the sun.

110   Landscapes of Andalucía

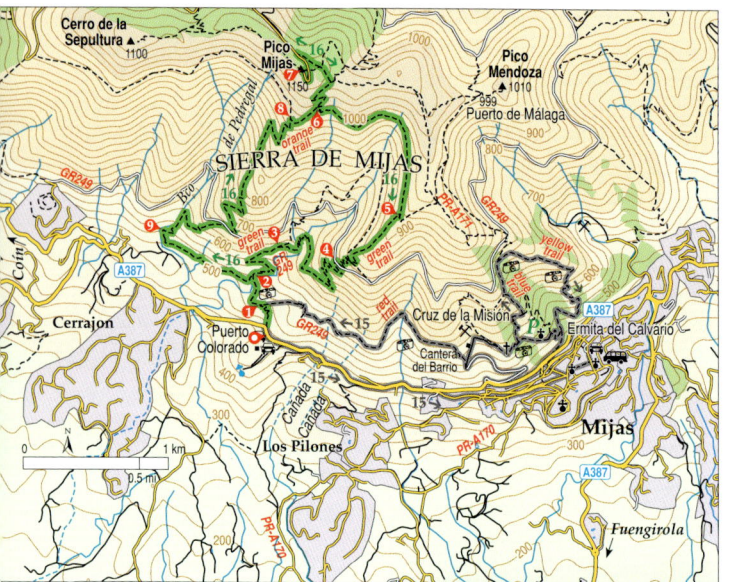

takes you across a rocky river bed, no doubt dry as a bone, the *bola* always on view.

You reach another JUNCTION (❻) for the final ascent: go right here on the orange trail; you will return on the same orange trail, heading left downhill. Passing more information panels, you cross another track and then meet the sealed lane to the peak. Follow it around a hairpin bend to the right and up to **Pico Mijas** (❼; 1150m/ 3772ft; **2-3h**). There is a trig point and several antennas, but the large white *bola* is owned by the state's meteorlogical agency. On a clear day, you can see Gibraltar and the Atlas Mountains in Morocco to the right, while to the left are Malaga and the mountains of the Sierra Nevada.

Fortify yourself here on the top for the steep descent! When you are ready, retrace your steps to ❻ (the JUNCTION where you first joined the orange trail). Go right here now. At the next JUNCTION (❽), go left. Put

Puerto Colorado

on the brakes! You descend the far side of the ridge in zigzags and in almost full sun this can be more tiring than the ascent. You touch on the forestry track again and follow it to the right before picking up your downward path. At the next JUNCTION (❾) turn left and descend through light tree cover to ❷, where you originally went right on the green trail. Descend some more, to the heavily signposted junction at ❶ and on to **Puerto Colorado** (**4-6h**).

Walk 17: MARBELLA • PUERTO DE MARBELLA • OLIVAR DE JUANAR • EL CEREZAL • OJEN

Distance: 10.8km/7mi; 4h23min
Grade: ●-● moderate-strenuous, with an ascent of 750m/2460ft (some of it steep and prolonged) and descent of 550m/1800ft. Paths and tracks are good, though some may be very wet after rain. The route is well waymarked throughout (yellow/white PR stripes, also some red/white GR249 waymarks from El Cerezal).
Equipment: see page 51.
How to get there: 🚌 town bus Linea 1 (every 20min); see plan of Marbella on the touring map. Get off at the first stop after crossing the *autovía*, behind the *Bomberos* (fire station) and walk about 700m/yds up to the Virgen del Carmen cemetery. Or go on foot: from the Plaza de Toros walk up the Ojén road, past the McDonald's roundabout, over the *autovía* (1.3km) and on to the cemetery (2.1km). Or 🚕 taxi or car to the cemetery. We prefer to drive to Ojén and get the 10.15 bus down to the cemetery, so that our car is waiting for us at the end of the walk.
To return: 🚌 from Ojén (Timetable 8) to the cemetery or on to the Marbella bus station (on the north side of the *autovía*, just west of the Ojén road), or 🚕 taxi.

Short walk: Mirador de Juanar
(3.4km/2.1mi; 1h). 🔵 Easy; ascent/descent of only 60m/200ft). Access by 🚗: turn left off the A355 just north of Ojén and drive 5km to the **Refugio de Juanar**. You can park here (adds about 20min to the overall walking time) or drive up a little further to a small car park (❹; 36° 34.709'N, 4°53.045'W). Walk straight up the dirt road and then gently ascend through the **Olivar de Juanar**, a vast olive grove. Continue to the *mirador* (❺; 35min; P17b) overlooked by a giant statue of an ibex and commanding views all the way down to Marbella.

Alternative walk: Ojén — Ermita de Juanar — El Cerezal — Ojén
(4.8km/3mi; 2h). ● Moderate, with an ascent (some of it steep) and corresponding descent of 350m/1150ft overall. Equipment as page 51, *plus torch for the long tunnels under the Ojén bypass road*. Access: 🚗 or 🚌 (Timetable 8) to/from Ojén; alight opposite the petrol station; park in the designated car park just past the petrol station. From the BUS STOP/PETROL STATION (❾) walk towards the centre for 40m/yds and climb shallow stone steps beside the VILLA LOLI, onto a rocky trail (red/white/yellow GR and PR waymarking). Wind high above the groves, keeping the village down on your right. At the end of a short rough section, go straight ahead on a concreted track which comes up from a *cortijo*. It's quite steep, but doesn't last long, soon levelling out and becoming a DIRT TRACK (12min). Up ahead is the Ojén bypass and behind it a pointed rocky peak under which you will pass later in the walk. Cross an *arroyo* and, just before the track enters an open area with *cortijos* on the right, turn up left on a narrow stony PATH, leaving the GR249 and now following yellow/white wayamarking (❽; 16min). Go over some boulders and into a TUNNEL under the bypass. Emerging from the tunnel, follow a small path straight ahead (SIGNPOSTED 'ERMITA JUANAR'; 21min). It immediately bears right and takes you through a METAL

111

GATE. This marks the start of a fairly steep trail which you will follow through pines for some time. Underfoot the ground is sandy or carpeted with pine needles. Droppings, footprints and disturbed soil provide ample evidence of the passage of animals, mostly *cabra montés*. As you pass under a huge CLIFF (50min), a sign points right, to the **Ermita de Juanar** (●C), an elaborately-decorated shrine built into the rock face. Back on the main trail, continue uphill and soon start zigzagging, passing the pointed rock you saw from below, Cerro Nicolás. Shortly after that, reach a JUNCTION (●6; 1h10min), where the MAIN WALK comes down from the left. Turn right, picking up the main walk at the 3h33min-point and following it back to Ojén.

This walk winds directly up to the Puerto de Marbella, a 906m/2970ft-high pass through the impressive Sierra Blanca. Close by are the ruins of the Refugio de Juanar, an old hunting lodge formerly frequented by kings and princes.

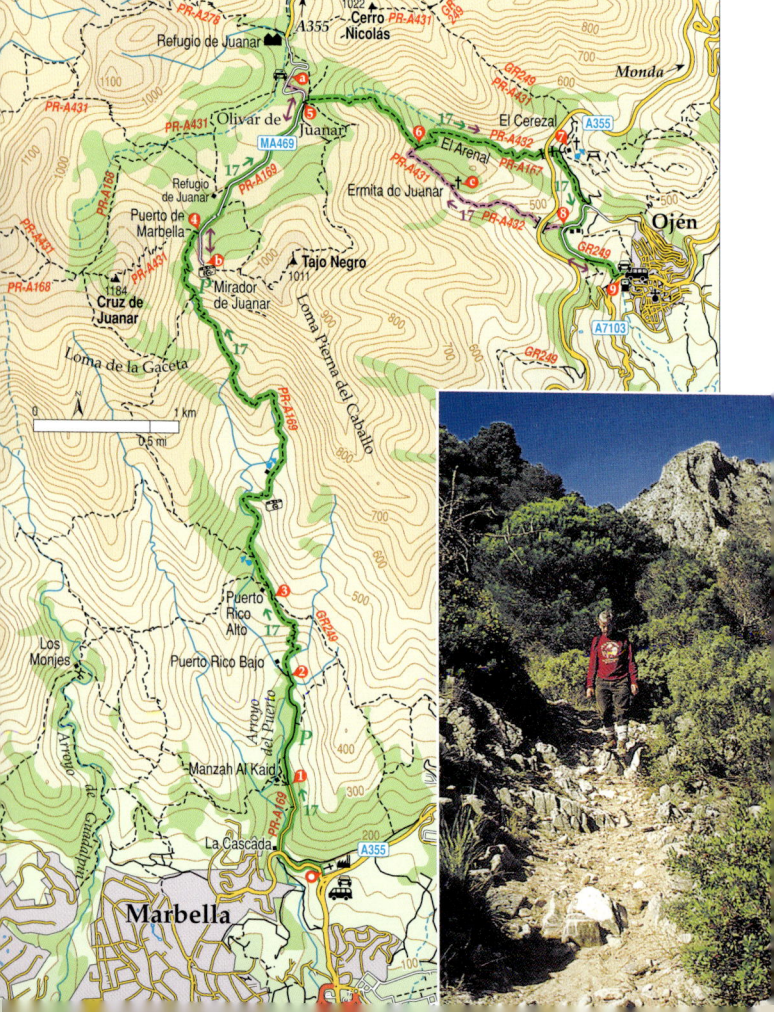

Walk 17: From Marbella to Ojén

The new *refugio* is now a *hotel parador*. Though steep, the climb is not difficult, and you will be so entranced by the amazing variety of trees, shrubs, herbs and wildflowers that you will scarcely be aware of any fatigue. If you are lucky you may spot an agile *cabra montés* and in this haven for birds, look out particularly for black wheatear on the lower slopes and black redstart higher up.

Start at the *cementerio* (the cemetery, *not* the cement works which just happens to be alongside it!). Take the road between the walled-in CEMETERY (●) and FINCA LA TORRECILLA, signposted to the 'Cascada' restaurant/bar. You will follow a stream, the **Arroyo del Puerto**, to its source just below the Puerto de Marbella. At a junction in front of the restaurant La Cascada (**4min**), turn right on a lane. The road surfacing disappears outside the entrance to the old **Finca Manzah Al Kaid** (❶; **13min**). Continue straight up a track, past a chain, towards crags and peaks ahead; a yellow/white WAYMARKING POST is on the right. You pass some flat open areas down by the STREAM (**16min**; *P*17a). When you next approach the water's edge (**30min**), the track becomes a rocky and stony trail. At a fork before the substantial working *cortijo* **Puerto Rico Bajo** (❷; **35min**), waymarking directs you to the right, towards Puerto Rico Alto. The trail narrows and, as you emerge from some woods, the crags tower directly ahead.

The next section of the trail doubles as a water run-off in rainy weather, so be prepared to paddle along, avoiding as much as you can. It leads up a couple of abandoned terraces to a point where an enclosed concrete *acequia* comes down from above. The path runs up the right-hand edge of the *acequia* but, if it is very wet, take a detour round to the right and join the *acequia* nearer the top, at a WHITE WATER CONTROL BLOCK (**44min**). This serves as a signpost, but the writing can be almost obscured by torrents of water.

Before continuing, look back. Marbella seems a long way off and already Finca Puerto Rico Bajo is far below you. Lose sight of the valley (**56min**) and wind round on a level stretch above the crags, past citrus groves sitting comfortably in a cultivated mountain plain. Just after passing a ruined *cortijo*, you cross an old *acequia* at **Puerto Rico Alto** (❸). If the path is flooded just climb over the roof of the water control block.

Once more in open woodland, go straight ahead for 'Juanar' at a junction (**1h05min**), where Los Monjes is signposted to the left. The gradient steepens as you come out of the woods into an area of low shrubs, bushes and bracken, and you'll see the Cruz de Juanar, the rocky peak directly ahead. There is no lack of opportunity to pause and rest, but one particularly delightful spot presents itself where the path has come very close to the stream again (**1h21min**). Oleanders overhang a pool of water beneath a huge rock, creating an attractive little corner.

The trail continues to wind up steeply, and Marbella comes into view again for a short time. Go into some pines and notice how

Photo opposite: near the end of the walk, with Cerro Nicolás in the background

sandy the soil is beneath the stones. The terrain becomes more rocky (**1h50min**) as you proceed to a CREST (**2h01min**), from where you can clearly see the pass, your target, ahead. After a short descent, you reach an open sandy area. Ignore the path going off left above a wide sloping rock face, and turn up right (**2h21min**).

The trail crosses an area of pale-coloured boulders, passes a path off left to the summit of Juanar (45min up, 25min down) and rises to the **Puerto de Marbella** (**❹**; **2h34min**) where, suddenly, the world looks different. You find yourself in a level pine wood, with a dirt road running just beyond it. The road to the right leads to a *mirador* overlooked by a spectacular statue of an ibex (target for the Short walk), but we turn left downhill, towards the triangular summit of Cerro Nicolás. Alongside the Centro de Recuperación e Investigación Cinegética, a hunting centre, magnificent chestnut trees front the ruins of the old hunting lodge, the **Refugio de Juanar** (**2h50min**). A little further on, extending along both sides of this motorable forestry track, is the **Olivar de Juanar**, a vast and still very productive olive grove. At the end of the grove (**3h08min**) the forestry road makes a sharp bend to the left. (The new Refugio de Juanar, a *parador,* lies some 15 minutes ahead.) Leave the road and turn off to the right just before the bend (**❺**; signpost, 'OJÉN 4KM' and white/yellow waymarks). Ignore two paths going to the left and take the one going straight ahead, at right angles to the road. It's an enchanting path, another old trail, quite steep with sandy soil and a carpet of pine needles making it mostly soft underfoot.

At a T-JUNCTION (**❻**; **3h33min**), the Ermita de Juanar is signed to the right *(the Alternative walk comes up here)*, but head left for 'CEREZAL, OJÉN'. Wind down into the valley past an 'EL ARENAL' SIGN, ravaged with time, which draws your attention to a particularly sandy slope (**3h40min**). Begin to follow a *barranco*, criss-crossing it several times before seeing the huge holding wall of the A355 Ojén bypass directly ahead. Go through a short TUNNEL (**3h53min**), across a grid and through a gate in the goat fence. Now another surprise awaits you: formerly a *cortijo*, **El Cerezal** (**❼**; **3h55min**) has been transformed into a charming *zona recreativa* set on several levels, with a shrine to Nuestra Señora del Pilar, a stream, and a tiny lemon grove – just the place for a short break.

A narrow road takes you downstream past cypress trees, to the MAIN ENTRY GATE. Go through and, almost immediately, wind round to the right at a JUNCTION (red/white/yellow WAYMARKING POST). Continue without turns to where *cortijos* sit to the left of an open area (**❽**; **4h09min**) at the foot of the slopes. Keep straight ahead on the main track (the path which goes up the slopes to the right is the outward route of the Alternative walk). Your motorable track is sometimes rough and rocky, sometimes concreted; as it bends sharply left, go straight ahead on a path. Just after meeting a narrow *acequia*, the path turns left, crosses the watercourse and descends to the road at the side of the Villa Loli. Turn right the short way to the PETROL STATION/BUS STOP in **Ojén** (**❾**; **4h23min**).

Walk 18: ISTAN

Distance: 8.3km/5.1mi; 2h09min
Grade: 🔴 moderate; a descent of 150m/495ft and corresponding ascent at the end of the walk. Mostly on good signposted and waymarked PR paths and tracks.
Equipment: see page 51
How to get there and return: 🚗 to/from Istán (the 15.5km-point in the Istán detour on Car tour 6); park in the car park at the village entrance (36° 34.847'N, 4°56.850'W). Or 🚌 (Timetable 9; infrequent)

Short walk: The essence of Istán (2km/1.2mi; 45min). 🔵 Easy, with a descent (some of it steep) and corresponding ascent of 50m/165ft at the end of the walk. Follow the main walk into the park and *zona recreativa*, and pause at the notice board describing the park's inception in November 1999. If you have time for a 20-minute return detour, continue following the main walk to **El Nacimiento** (❶; *P*18a) — it's worth the effort. Just beyond the notice board, ignore a narrow path down to the left and take the wide steps that descend a little further along. Turn right at a junction and continue downwards to meet an *acequia*. Cross it and carry on descending on a very steep narrow path (trekking pole useful). Turn left when you meet a concrete track (14min) and notice a stone bridge below, the return route of the main walk. Pass above orchards of citrus fruit, avocados, apricots and peaches and reach the village outskirts (20min). Go up the

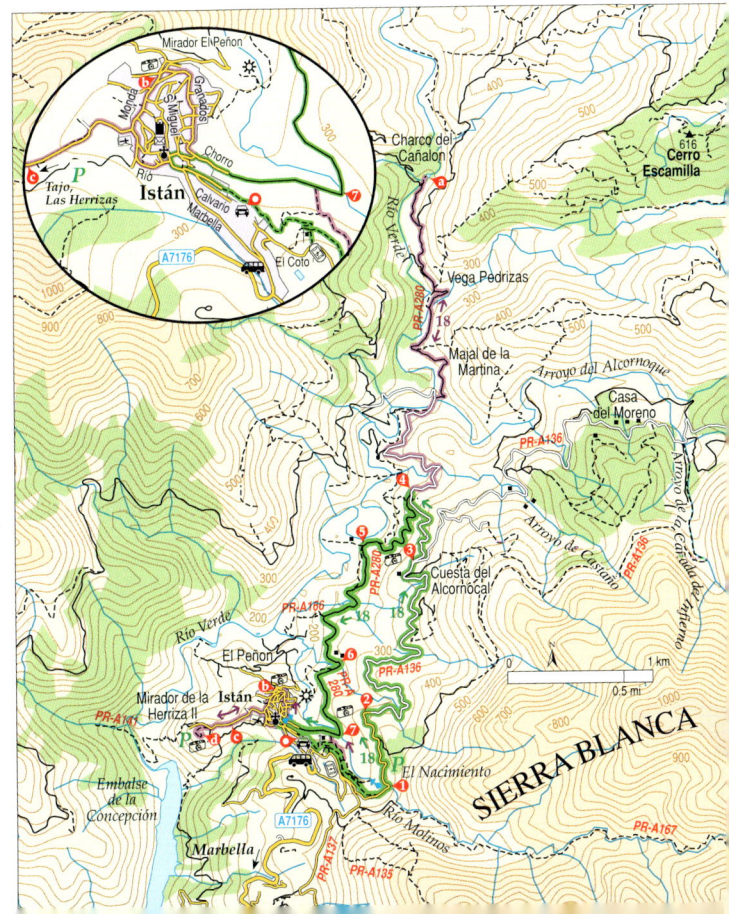

concreted street and bear right, around the edge of the village, passing from Calle del Chorro to Calle de los Granados. *Chorro* means both a sword, the emblem of Istán, and a water jet — and water is one of the main features of this village. Skirt around, keeping level, through the colourfully attractive narrow streets. Just beyond Casa Verde you reach a viewpoint, the **Mirador de El Peñón** b, which offers panoramic views over the valley of the Río Verde (24min). Continuing on from the *mirador*, fork left and ascend a little, then follow Calle de la Monda round to the CEMETERY. From here signs direct you to 'Tajo Banderas' and 'Las Herrizas'. Follow the signs and head up to the right, on a little esplanade lined with bougainvillaea, citrus and palm trees. You pass a first viewpoint, **Tajo Banderas** c, with an orientation table showing the names of the surrounding peaks. But continue further on the beautifully paved trail to a three-way fork, where you go straight ahead *past* a *mirador* on the left to the **Mirador de la Herriza II** (d; 36min, *P*18b), with its splendid view over the Embalse de la

Fuente El Chorro in the centre of Istán, with its seven spouts

Concepción. In the mornings and evenings, the village elders look out across the valley and contemplate the wonders of nature and the meaning of life. Return to the cemetery and head right on Calle del Río, to the CHURCH SQUARE. Turn right and pause to admire the decorative village *lavadero* and *fuente* shown opposite, then continue uphill on Calle del Calvario to the car park (45min).

Alternative walk: Charco del Canalón (15.7km/9.7mi; about 4h40min). ● Moderate; grade as main walk, with an extention of constant undulations of about 60m/200ft; all signposted and waymarked. Keep straight on along the PR-A280 at ❹. All the turnings are well signposted, and there are WAYMARKING POSTS. You pass a couple of isolated *cortijos* and eventually see a DILAPIDATED SUSPENSION BRIDGE on the left — used by locals when the river is running really high. Ford the **Río Verde** (a sign warns of danger at this ford) and take the signposted path to the **Charco del Canalón** (❹) with its waterfall. Take care if you are not a swimmer! Return the same way.

Much of the melting snow from the high peaks in the Parque Natural Sierra de las Nieves drains into the Río Verde and collects in the Embalse de la Concepción, just west of Marbella. Istán sits above the northern tip of the reservoir, and this circular walk takes you from there into the southern region of the park. The abundance of water creates a series of fertile mountain valleys between slopes which support a huge variety of trees and shrubs. The scenery is always magnificent but, after the winter snows, when the peaks are dazzlingly-white, it is even more splendid.

Begin the walk at the CAR PARK in Istán (❍): follow the steep road (Calle del Calvario) up towards the 'Polideportivo' (sports complex). Fork left after a few minutes into the El Coto *zona recreativa* and take the attractive stone-paved path along the edge of an *acequia*. *(The Short walk turns down steps here.)* When the paving ends, continue beside the *acequia* on a narrow, somewhat eroded (but yellow/white waymarked) path which runs below an enclosure, after which a short concrete stretch will take you back up to the road. Either way, turn left and pass **El Nacimiento** (❶; **15min**, *P*18a), an imaginatively landscaped area at the SOURCE of the **Río Molinos**.

Continue on a yellow/white-waymarked narrow road, the PR-A136 (also a cycling route to Monda), contouring under the western slopes of the Sierra Blanca. The gradient is fairly gradual, with just one or two steeper parts, and the easy walking enables you to relax and enjoy the delightful views that greet you around every bend.

Ignore a sign pointing to the waymarked Sendero Cañada del Infierno off to the right, and then a rough track off right. As the road veers right (❷; **38min**), ignore a concreted track going steeply back left to a *cortijo* on the lower slopes. Around November, olive trees growing along the verge are laden with fruit of differing colours. Eventually the asphalt peters out and you're on a smooth stabilised

El Nacimiento, the spring 15min into the walk (Picnic 18a); below: custard apples are cultivated in some of the orchards.

dirt road. Close to a white house a track comes in from the right off the **Cuesta del Alcornocal** (Cork Oak Hill; **58min**). Two minutes later, at a heavily signposted JUNCTION (**❸**; **1h**), fork down left on a good track affording fantastic views into the Río Verde Valley.

Pass under cables and reach another JUNCTION (**❹**; **1h10min**). The main walk turns sharp left here on Cycle route 6. *(The Alternative walk goes straight ahead; but you do not have to follow the alternative to the charco: you could just follow the track close to the* river upstream as far as you like, returning the same way.

Just 100m after PR-A280 has joined from the right, you pass a track down to a *cortijo* on the right (**❺**; **1h23min**). Leaving the cables behind, the track takes you up through orchards of citrus fruits, avocados and *chirimoyas* (custard apples). Notice some interesting rocky pinnacles on the right.

When you reach a STEEP SECTION (**❻**; **1h46min**) take it easy, keeping an eye open for the old mill down in the valley. Ignore the tracks coming in from some properties and follow a concrete section of track across a bridge over the **Río Molinos**. Entering **Istán** (**2h01min**), turn up left and round to the CHURCH SQUARE. Go left alongside a bar and up steep Calle del Calvario at the right of the **Fuente del Chorro**. This leads directly into the CAR PARK in **Istán** (**2h09min**).

Walk 19: RIO DEL BURGO

See also photo on page 41
Distance: 19km/11.8mi; 4h45min
Grade: ● strenuous (because of the length), with ascents/descents of 330m/1080ft overall. Almost entirely along a motorable track; PR marked in the first half
Equipment: see page 51.
How to get there and return: 🚗 to/from El Burgo, the 86km-point on Car tour 6 (or drive directly from Marbella via Coín); park near the bridge over the Río del Burgo on the southern outskirts of the village (36°47.356'N, 4°56.964'W).

Shorter walk: The 'cathedral' (13km/8mi; 3h20min). ● Easy, with a gentle ascent/descent of 150m/490ft. Access and equipment as main walk. Follow the main walk to ❹ (the 1h40min-point — our 'cathedral with organ pipes') and return the same way.

Short walks: ● both are easy; access and equipment as main walk.

1 To the first weir and reservoir (4km/2.5mi; 1h15min). Gentle ascent/descent of only about 50m/165ft. Follow the main walk to ❶ (the 38min-point) and return the same way.

2 El Burgo — La Fuensanta — El Burgo (6km/3.7mi; 1h38min). Ascent and corresponding descent of 100m/330ft *each way*. Follow the main walk to the 4min-point at **Villa El Quinto Pino**. Turn left on a steep signposted track just past it (which has unfortunately obliterated an old stony trail — the ancient route linking El Burgo with Fuensanta). When wet, the muddy clay of the surfacing can be a nuisance. Climb between cultivated fields and olive groves and walk along a couple of level terraces. Once out on the slopes (20min), take time to look back into the valley. Continue upwards, forking right onto what is left of the old trail, marked by CAIRNS (26min). Reach a crest, the **Puerto de los Lobos** (❾; Wolves' Pass; 31min) and descend straight ahead. Take any one of several paths through the pines (but make sure you keep to the right of the main watercourse), until the single path eventually becomes more obvious. Pass a deep ravine dropping away on your left (41min), and after alternate steep and level stretches you will see **Fuensanta** below. The path will take you down to the track at a STONE CROSS (❽; 49min), just to the right of the old MILL AND PICNIC AREA. Return the same way; if necessary, follow the main walk from the 4h-point.

S et in the northern region of the Parque Natural Sierra de las Nieves, this river walk is delightful at any time of year. Tits, black redstarts and other small birds are plentiful, and colour is provided by wildflowers in spring and the rich reds and golds of the trees in autumn. And although the charming *zona recreativa* of Fuensanta may be teeming with visitors at weekends and *fiestas*, at other times it is blissfully tranquil. And after your walk, take time to look around the attractive village of El Burgo, with its hilltop church of Santa Maria.

Start out from the Yunquera side of the old BRIDGE across the **Río del Burgo** (⓿). Take the track down off the road (info board, GR243 signpost) and, with the river on your right, follow it upstream through cultivated fields and olive groves. A very gradual

120 Landscapes of Andalucía

incline takes you past the **Villa El Quinto Pino** (**4min**); the signposted track just past it will be your return route; keep right here. (*But Short walk 2 turns left.*) Your track, now some metres above river level, heads towards the hills. Pines grow on the slopes while deciduous trees line the river banks.

At the first of several weirs (❶; **31min**), water cascades from a reservoir down into a lagoon, a popular bathing spot in summer. A rocky promontory overlooks the weir, and a narrow chained-off track goes down to the waterside and another lagoon (**38min**; *P*19a), goal of Short walk 1. Continue on the main track, ignoring another which crosses the river to a small *molino* (mill) further along.

The valley narrows for a while, with cliffs on the left. A *cortijo* on the opposite bank is particularly pretty in autumn (**44min**), and curious pyramid-shaped structures stand outside another *cortijo*, in ruins at the side of the track. Climb quite high above the river and, after passing a deep side-gorge (**54min**), look out for a very sheer, orange-coloured section of cliff. Perched on top, overlooking another WEIR (❷; **58min**) and reservoir, is the white monument at the Mirador del Guarda Forestal on the road between El Burgo and Ronda.

The river flows through a deep, narrow channel far below as you enjoy a fairly straight and level section (**1h20min**), before descending a little, then rising past a *casita* with animal shelters (**Cortijo de Hierba Buena**; ❸; **1h29min**). Set above yet

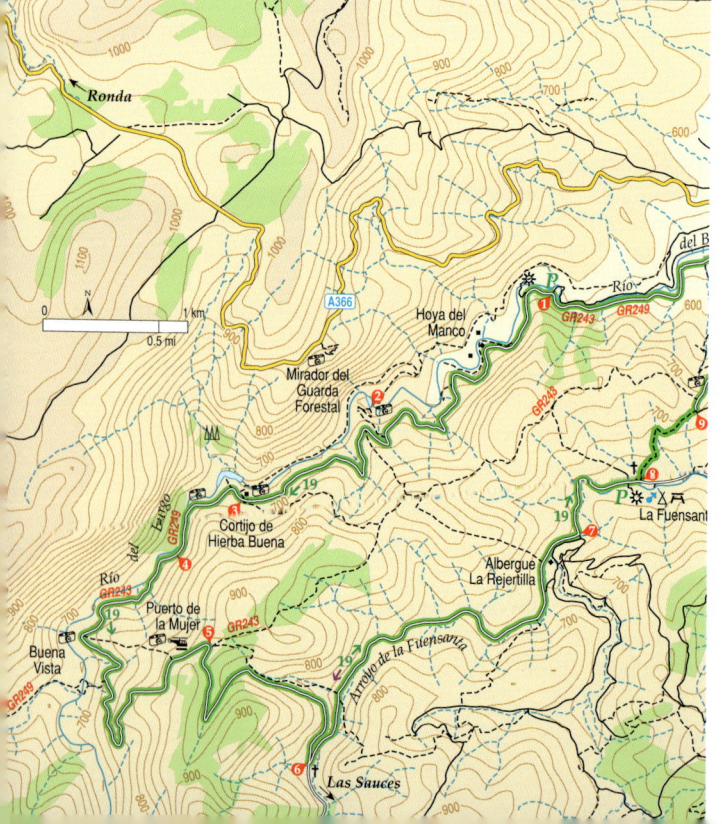

Walk 19: Río del Burgo

another weir and protected by noisy but harmless little dogs, it is just used for the daily tending of sheep and goats. Soon (**1h35min**) you're in the setting shown overleaf, passing above clear, sparkling lagoons overlooked by a spectacular rugged outcrop which, from a little further on, resembles a 'cathedral' tiered with organ pipes. There's another charming spot down at RIVER LEVEL (❹; **1h40min**), pleasant for a pause on the pebbly banks or in the shade of pines. *(The Shorter walk turns back here.)*

Up to this point the track has been gently undulating, but it now begins to climb steadily. Stop for breath as the track turns left and contemplate the valley that opens out on the right (**1h52min**). Encircled by mountains, and wooded with pines, it is traversed by a deep gorge running between steep and pronounced cliffs — the ongoing route of the GR243. The upstream section of the river and the GR waymarking are left behind when another left-hand bend (**2h11min**) takes you back, high above your original route, through trees which provide cooling shade for a while. Emerging into the open again, pause briefly for a view back through the gorge (**2h23min**) and take a welcome rest when you reach **Puerto de la Mujer** (❺; Woman's Pass; **2h30min**).

Now the long but pleasant descent begins. Views are dominated by the rugged silhouette of Prieta (1521m), and on the ground you might see giant mushrooms, especially in autumn and winter. A tall STONE CROSS marks a junction with a forestry track (❻; **3h01min**), where Las Sauces, a camping area, is some 3km to the right. Turn left and follow the **Arroyo de la Fuensanta** downstream. There's still a long way to go, but it's almost all downhill through delightful shady woodland. Sunlight filters through the trees and the sound of running water and birdsong keeps you company. Pass a track crossing the river to the large **Albergue La Rejertilla** (❼; **3h39min**).

Just as you enter **La Fuensanta**, there is a track up to the left, marked by another tall STONE CROSS (❽; **4h**). This is your onward route, but first explore this delightful *zona recreativa* built around an old mill (***P**19b*). Then turn up the PR-waymarked track by the cross but, almost immediately, cut off right on a path (indistinct at first) which runs up alongside an olive grove. The

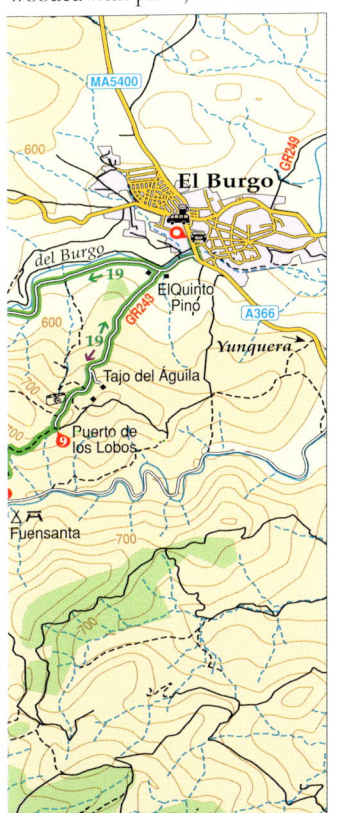

122 Landscapes of Andalucía

path, CAIRN-marked, becomes more obvious and wider as it winds up through pines, then levels to contour around the slopes. At a fork, where there is a deep *barranco* on the right, take either path (the path to the left is a little less steep).

Climb round and rise to a crest, the **Puerto de los Lobos** (9); Wolves' Pass), from where El Burgo can be seen in the valley below. Now descend on a stony old trail, through olive groves and cultivated fields. It soon becomes a track which leads you down to your outward route on the banks of the **Río del Burgo**. Turn right and follow the track to the BRIDGE and your car (**4h45min**).

Lagoon below the 'cathedral'

Walk 20: PEÑÓN DE LOS ENAMORADOS (LOVERS' ROCK)

See also photo on pages 6-7
Distance: 12km/7.4mi; 4h40min. Allow an extra half hour if you wish to climb the Enamorados peak.
Grade: ● strenuous, with ascents/descents of 500m/1640ft overall. On one section there is no defined path: care is needed in navigation. PR waymarking/signposting from ❼, green/white SL waymarking from the Puerto de los Pilones
Equipment: see page 51; *walking boots and compass or GPS essential*
How to get there and return: 🚗 to/from the Quejigales entrance to the Parque Natural Sierra de las Nieves between the KM13 and KM14 road markers on the A397 (the 47km-point on Car tour 6; signposted 'Conejeras 300m' and 'Los Quejigales 10km'). Drive along the dirt road, where peonies bloom in May, past the Conejeras area (marked by a board; *P*CT6). Ford a usually-dry watercourse and immediately fork left. Fences, grids and gates control the passage of the *cabra montés*. (The main gate is usually open, *but you will have to walk an extra 3km each way if it is closed without notice, beware!*) Veer left at Cortijo Las Navas and follow the road as it winds up, becoming partially surfaced (5.5km) with some potholes and unprotected drops. Ignore the right turn to Puerto de las Golondrinas (6km) and reach a Y-fork (9km), where right leads to the signposted Puerto de los Pilones. Go left to the Quejigales camping/picnic area (10km) and park in the enclosure at the ranger's building or just beyond it (36° 41.430'N, 5°2.732'W).

Short walk: Fuente del Pinar (4km/2.5mi; 1h). ● Easy, with an ascent/descent of 130m/425ft, all on tracks. Access and equipment as main walk. Follow the main walk to ❷ (31min) and retrace steps.

Alternative walk: Puerto de los Pilones (7.5km/4.7mi; 2h30min). Strenuous, with an ascent/descent of 450m/1475ft. Access and equipment as main walk, but GPS/compass not essential. From the Quejigales building walk back along the dirt road and take the dirt road up to the left (10min). Pass through a chain barrier and start the long but gentle, winding climb, pausing for breath at a viewpoint (20min). Gorse, then pines, accompany you as far as a sharp bend to the left (1411m; 28min). Continue in full sunlight until you pass under a few shady *pinsapos* (48min). You will marvel at the sierras lined up one behind the other in almost every direction. Then the whole Quejigales area and Cortijo Las Navas come into view (1h05min). The walk continues down a steep path to the left (1h21min), but it's worth continuing for about 150m to the **Puerto de los Pilones**. Then pick up the main walk at the 3h33min-point and descend rather more steeply to your car.

It is essential to choose a clear, calm day to get the best out of this exhilarating and highly-satisfying mountain walk in the heart of the park. Make sure you are properly equipped for the conditions. From January to March, snow can drift up to a metre deep on the slopes of Enamorados and, at other times, the altitude can mean scorching sun or very chilly temperatures. But it's always beautiful. The sight of the cushions of hedgehog broom, spines encased in ice, sparkling like jewels in the brilliant sunshine of mid-November, is never to be forgotten. The start of spring heralds a different spectacle, with the *pinsapos* sprouting bright green buds from the ends of every branch, and wildflowers begin to carpet the hillsides. As for wildlife, apart from the beautiful horses that roam free in the park, you are quite likely to spot small herds of ibex and, if you are lucky, a *meloncillo* or North African mongoose.

Start out from the *área recreativa* **Quejigales** (**O**) by going along the motorable track past the picnic benches and camping area. Pass through a chain barrier, to an INFORMATION PANEL which marks your return path across the stream from Puerto de los Pilones on the SL-A140 (**5min**). Ignore a track off left to a water tank a minute later. Continue upstream along the track, on a gradual incline, through fragrant pine woods. Shortly after the track veers right into open grassy countryside (**15min**), pines begin to be replaced by the distinctive shapes and darker foliage of *pinsapos*. A Y-fork marks the **Puerto de Quejigales** (**❶**; **16min**): head right here on a forestry track (when last surveyed, this run was *not signposted*). You circle under towering cliffs (keeping left at the next Y-fork), to the **Fuente del Pinar** (**❷**; **26min**) on the left (also called the Fuente de Molina). Up to the right, a STONE MONUMENT commemorates a ranger who devoted his life to protecting the *pinsapo*. Soon the track deteriorates into a rough path and crosses a little GULLY (**❸**; **31min**), with retaining walls to prevent erosion up to the right. Ignore paths left and right — if you even notice them; again, there is no signpost. *(The Short walk turns back here.)*

The path starts to climb steadily; continue circling uphill below the crags. Remember to take it easy at this altitude. The local people say you should '*subir como un viejo, para llegar como un joven*' — 'climb like an old man, to arrive like a youngster'. **Attention:** About 650m/yds past the gully you arrive at a Y-fork above the **Mirador de los Coloraillos**, where the right-hand fork (the main route, via the Cañada de las Ánimas) may be still marked with blue paint. Be sure to go *left* here (**❹**) on a somewhat lesser trail (*not waymarked*). Now in *pinsapo* woodland, look out for short-toed tree creepers and the ibex that often gather here. Through the trees, notice the barren rocky mass of the Sierra de la Hidalga (1407m) over to the left (northwest) — and a vast limestone wall of rock ahead (**46min**). Contemplating the magnificent and ancient *pinsapos* that form this area of woodland, it is easy to understand why they are accorded special status.

Descend gradually through the wood, to a point where Cerro Alto looms ahead through a gap (**50min**). To its left, and perhaps best described as a hemispherical rocky dome, is your goal, the isolated peak of Enamorados. Beyond a couple of CLEARINGS

Walk 20: Peñón de los Enamorados

(**54min**) the path steepens, winding down to run along the base of a rocky slope on the right, through some prickly shrubbery and across rocks. A CAVE is set into the rock face (**Cueva de Manijero; 1h06min**) not long before the massive bulk of the LIMESTONE WALL comes into sight again, now just ahead.

There is another Y-fork just before the wall: the main path (to the Peñón de Ronda) goes left here, circling to the left of the limestone mass. *Your* ongoing path (**5**), a little indistinct, rises up the right-hand side of the wall over rocks and stones and, passing to the left of a CAIRN, it soon comes alongside a watercourse. Water sometimes flows strongly here, giving birth to delightful little waterfalls, but often there may be scarcely a trickle. When you see a STONE TROUGH on the opposite bank, to the left, cross over to it (**1h20min**). Pause to refill water bottles from the *fuente* which keeps it topped up, and rest before the next stage of the climb.

From the top end of the trough climb up diagonally to the right. There is a path of sorts, but you are likely to keep losing it. Although the slope is steep it's quite easy going as you just head upwards across the rocks, picking your way between low gorse bushes. Head roughly northeast, towards the left-hand end of the saddle you see ahead; when last seen, this was well cairned. Zigzagging eases the gradient and, passing to the left of a rocky shoulder, you should eventually locate the reasonable path which takes you on to the grassy saddle, the **Puerto del Canalizo** at almost 1600m (**6**; **1h49min**). Before picking up the narrow path that runs along it to the right, take a moment in this lovely spot to absorb the extensive views which greet you. Just below, steep cliffs drop into the valley; ahead are the lakes of El Chorro, near Antequera; round to the left is the Sierra de Grazalema (Walks 21-23); and, to the right, Enamorados rises alongside Cerro Alto.

Here you see the first of the hedgehog broom, a low spiny cushion-like shrub which carpets much of the next part of the route. Characteristic of the highest mountains of southern Europe and North Africa, it usually grows between 1700m and 2000m, sometimes called the 'hedgehog zone'. Interspersed with the broom are the distinctive dark spiky leaves and bulbous light green flowers of the unfortunately-named, but eyecatching, stinking hellebore.

Set off, following the path as it heads round the far side of the closest hill (roughly east-southeast) and climbs diagonally up its bare rocky slope, home to noisy choughs. The path crosses a small gully (**2h01min**) and heads upwards to a CREST (**2h08min**). Follow it straight ahead towards the next ridge, with Enamorados rising majestically over to the right. As you skirt a rock wall on the left and cross an open expanse of grassy slope (**2h16min**), you come upon a wonderful sight — suddenly the whole of this book is laid out before you. From left to right almost every sierra is visible, from Grazalema all the way round to the magnificent Sierra Nevada. For much of the year this latter at least will be snow-capped, adding to the fairytale panorama. We have seldom seen such an awe-inspiring view; *now* you realise why we recommended a clear day.

When you are ready to move on, continue eastwards (straight towards the Sierra Nevada) along the path for 20-30 metres, but turn sharp right at a WAYMARKING POST with the yellow/white flashes of the PR-A351 (**7**; **2h30min**). This trail crosses a stony slope and climbs to run along the Enamorados ridge. Cerro Alto rises beyond the dome, and the Torrecilla ridge is across to the left. Its main peak, the highest point in the park (1919m/6295ft), rises at the right-hand end of the ridge. Just below, looking almost dead, semi-evergreen oaks grow in a sloping *nava* (grassy mountain plain). These are the first of the many *quejigos*, Portuguese oaks, from which the area derives its name.

The path takes us down to the left of the rocky dome of **Enamorados** (1780m). However, if you are keen to conquer the peak (about 20m/65ft of scrambling) or to just sit on the rocks beneath the dome, leave the path and cut off to the right here (**2h34min**). It's as good a picnic spot as you'll find anywhere, with views extending over more meadows of *quejigos* to the Sierra de Mijas and the coast.

Continuing, the path heads round above the *quejigos,* leaving Enamorados behind. Bear left to a grassy patch and, after going over

This well-restored nevera *(snow pit), the Pozo de Nieve de Tolox, is passed at about 3h30min. It was used to collect snow which was compacted and cut into ice blocks — the old form of refrigeration.*

a rise, watch out for the deep unprotected CAVERN to the right of the path (**2h50min**). Cairns line the path as it passes across rocks and descends to a dip, from where several indistinct paths snake up the other side. Just head uphill and across the saddle ahead, to a FLAT AREA where water often collects (**3h04min**). The path is clear again and takes you through large clumps of heather, to a LARGE CAIRN in a small clearing. Head right, passing close to some *quejigos* which, one November, gave us quite a shower, when the ice encrusted on their branches melted in the afternoon sunshine.

Ignore the PR-A351 heading left to the summit of Torrecilla — a popular, but we think boring, walk, frequented by the locals on Sundays. Keep right here (**❽**, **3h10min**). Continue climbing and pass the huge *nevera* shown above, the **Pozo de Nieve de Tolox**. Notice the water control walls across streams down on the left, and continue across a grassy expanse under a relay tower and up to the track at the **Puerto de los Pilones** (**3h33min**). Views across the sierras are magnificent and, on a clear day, you'll see Gibraltar and the North African coast.

Turn left down the track, but leave it in under 200m: take a signposted path (**❾**) which descends to the right. It zigzags down open slopes through the **Cañada del Cuerno** (Horn Ravine; photo on pages 6-7), becoming steeper as it passes through a forest of *pinsapos* (the huge roots of these trees provide convenient footholds on the long descent). Once out of the trees (**4h16min**), Quejigales is visible below and the rocky slopes give way to an often-muddy area through pines. A wooden bridge takes you across the STREAM and on to the track at the INFO PANEL that you passed on the way out. Turn left, pass the **Quejigales** campsite and reach your car (**4h40min**).

Walk 21: GRAZALEMA • MERENDERO DEL BOYAR • LLANO DE LAS PRESILLAS • LLANO DEL ENDRINAL • GRAZALEMA

See also photo on page 45
Distance: 6.5km/4mi; 2h36min
Grade: ● moderate, with ascents/descents of 350m/1150ft overall (some steep sections). Some care with navigation may required in places, if signposts or waymarking posts are missing.
Equipment: See page 51; *walking boots essential; GPS track helpful*

How to get there and return: 🚗 to/from Camping Tajo Rodillo (the 88km-point on Car tour 7); park at the campsite (36° 45.571'N, 5°22.456'W). Or 🚐 to/from Grazalema (Timetable 10): the last bus stop is the village is by the campsite; ask the driver for Camping Tajo Rodillo.

This is an exhilarating walk which contrasts the gentleness of a river valley and a mountain meadow with the Llano de las Presillas, a wild and remote plain covered with sharp karstic rocks eroded by the elements. In late spring and summer these same rocks provide anchor and shade for delicate wildflowers.

Start out from the ENTRANCE TO CAMPSITE TAJO RODILLO (⊙) and walk up the road for just over 250m/yds. At the **Río Guadalete** (**5min**), sometimes dry at this point, take the CAMINO PEATONAL (pedestrian way) — the CAMINO DE LOS CHARCONES, which one 'Landscaper' has described as a 'motorway-standard footpath'. This has, unfortunately, replaced the gently-ascending zigzags of the

old meandering narrow paths and cobbled trails, so that walkers now have a more direct — but considerably steeper — route. But enjoy the birdsong which accompanies you and the oleanders which line the river bank. If you're lucky the river may even be flowing. Be grateful for the pines which provide occasional shade on the steep climb.

When you reach the **Merendero del Boyar** picnic shelter (**❶**; **45min**), go through the gate to its left. Follow the signpost and INFO BOARD for 'SENDERO PUERTO DE LAS PRESILLAS' straight ahead, past a GATE ('Zona de Reserva') and onto a straightforward, but fairly steep and rough, rocky path. At the top of the slope (**54min**) it bends right and passes through a gentle area of grass and pines (*P*21). You pass a LIME KILN on the right (**❷**; **Calera del Navaro**). The path then becomes stony for a while, as it runs alongside rocks on the left and climbs steeply. Views open up over the valley ahead (**1h06min**).

Keep following ARROWED WAYMARKING POSTS across a level grassy stretch, dotted with sharp karstic rocks (*lapiaces,* or 'labyrinths' according to an INFO PANEL), eventually rising between boulders. The path becomes faint at **Llano de las Presillas** (**❸**; **1h15min**), but there are signposts indicating Grazalema and the Puerto del Boyar. As you relax here and enjoy the scenery, note the twin peaks of Simancón and Reloj slightly to your left, identifiable by the scree slope below them.

Then bear right across the plain (ARROWED WAYPOSTS) until you can see a FENCE on top of a wall ahead. Some 150m/yds before the wall, you come to a signposted junction at the **Puerto de las Prisillas** (**❹**). A path forks off right to Benaocaz, but you fork left on a narrow but clear path which heads towards a rocky buttress on a scree slope. Several paths make their way down the valley at this stage, but if you stick to the main one as you pass below the buttress, you should see a *nevera* on the right (**❺**; a snow pit; **1h20min**) and another a short way further on. All the paths eventually converge on the main one which heads further down into the valley.

After a fairly rough descent (take care, it's ankle twisting terrain), the valley narrows and you find yourself on its left-hand side. After going through a CATTLE GATE (**❻**) you find yourselves at the start of a pleasant path

Grazalema, with Peñón Grande in the background

Peñón Grande

rounds the meadow, keeping the meadow on your right. At the corner of the fence, with a TROUGH and FUENTE above, go diagonally through trees and then pick up a clear narrow path which bears left for 'GRAZALEMA' (**8**; **2h01min**). It eventually heads towards **Peñón Grande**, home to booted eagles, which you'll see soaring around here from March to September.

At the top of the rise, the flat-topped mountain in the distance is the appropriately named Las Mesas (the Tables). As the path bears right and descends steeply again, always keep close to the towering rocks on the left and notice Grazalema and its separate Villa Turistica below (**2h09min**). Cross a gentler area of rocks and pines and then a long-disused *era* (**9**; **2h25min**) before an area of ramshackle dwellings. Go through a GATE ('Zona de Reserva'; **2h31min**), then reach **Camping Tajo Rodillo** (**2h36min**). This is the 'official' start of this hike; we do it in reverse to make the initial climb more gentle.

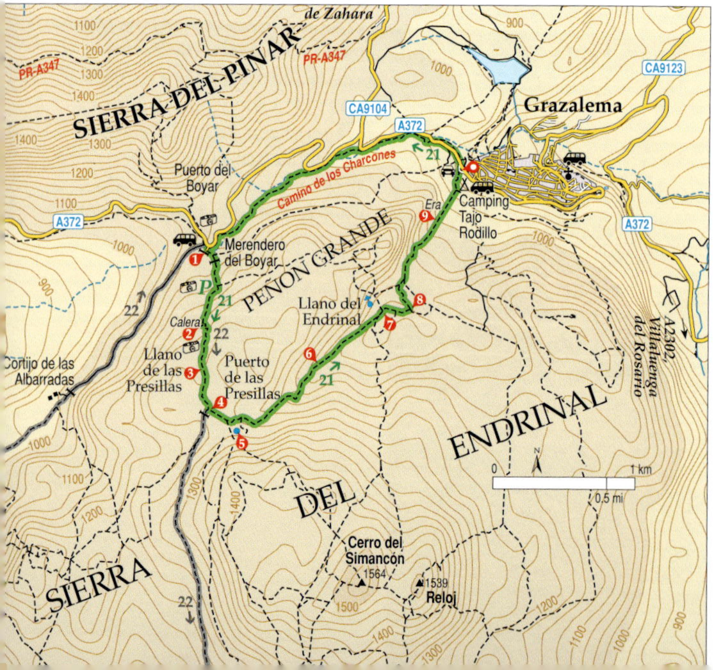

(**1h41min**); keep your eyes open for ibex and deer on the slopes, or for sheep grazing or sunning themselves.

The **Llano del Endrinal** (**7**; **1h52min**), a pine-covered, fenced meadow where they used to grow cereal crops, soon comes into view below, situated at the foot of the sheer cliffs of Peñón Grande. At a fork, take the narrow path which

Walk 22: BENAOCAZ • CASA DEL DORNAJO • PUERTO DE DON FERNANDO • SALTO DEL CABRERO • BENAOCAZ

The main walk begins on page 134; the map is overleaf.
Important note: This classic walk traditionally begins at the Puerto del Boyar. But in March 2014 the owners of the Cortijo de las Albarradas closed their land to walkers. Whether the track is public or private land is in dispute, but it appears that the *cortijo* owners have full maintenance responsibility, despite some 2000 walkers a month — many with dogs — using it. They have asked the council/park authorities for financial help, but in the current economic climate that is unlikely to be forthcoming. So for the past 10 years the only way to the Salto del Cabrero, *officially,* is from Benaocaz — as an out-and-back walk or a circuit which we describe on page 134. But we have also included the Oldfields' original walk — in case the route from the Puerto del Boyar opens in future.

Distance: 13.2km/8.2mi; 4h35min
Grade: ● moderate, with ascents/descents of 400m/1310ft overall, *but most of the walk is not signposted or waymarked at time of writing!*
Equipment: See page 51; *walking boots and compass or GPS essential*
How to get there and return: 🚗 to/from Benaocaz (the 52km-point on Car tour 7); park in the village (36° 42.004'N, 5°25.327'W) and make your way to the nearby church. Or 🚌 to/from Benaocaz (Timetable 10): the bus stop is on the A2302 near the church.
Short walks: Equipment as page 51; access as main walk
1 Arroyo del Pajaruco (4km/2.5mi; 1h18min). ● Easy, despite the ascent and corresponding descent of 260m/850ft. Follow the main walk to the WALL (❶; 28min). Do not go through the gate, but walk along the wall to the left and scramble through a GAP IN THE STONE WALL ahead. Turn right up a narrow earthen path, following a FENCE up to a GAP IN ANOTHER STONE WALL. Several narrow paths, really just animal tracks, fan out from here across a rocky meadow. Take a central one and bear left across the middle of the meadow towards trees and a line of rocks at the other side (about 200m away). The tall rock at the end of the line leans to the left, and this is the way you must go, just before reaching it. Walk down the GRASSY SLOPE (35min) and as it ends, step down right, on to the start of a rocky PATH (39min). As it passes through an overgrown section, you'll cross a little STREAM BED and both see and hear the **Arroyo del Pajaruco** far below on the right. Follow one of several paths, again mostly animal trails, which follow its direction downstream. Pass an animal TROUGH (46min) and come to the start of a long wall of rock. Follow the path, now clear, through an area of gorse, brilliantly coloured for many months of the year, and enjoy spectacular views across to the sierras in the far distance. The little conical huts of Los Chozos (hotel/apartments) appear down to the right, and then the rural plain below Benaocaz opens up. Reach the outskirts of the village at the POSADA EL PARRAL (1h09min) and carry straight on to the CHURCH (1h18min).

2 Salto del Cabrero (7.5km/4.7mi; 2h38min). ● Easy, with ascents/descents of 180m/590ft. This is the end of the main walk, in reverse. From the CHURCH (⭕) make your way along the main street to the north end of the village, where you'll find the SAN ANTON apartments/restaurant REFUGIO ANGÉLICA in a little square. Walk to the left of this building and, after passing an INFO PANEL about the *salto* and going through a GATE, descend the cobbled trail, to cross the little stone bridge across the **Arroyo del Pajaruco** (**9**; 24min, *P*22). Your path continues through another GATE and runs alongside a WALL in a grassy field (34min). Cross the field and start climbing on a winding, rocky trail, steep and sometimes cobbled. Go through a GATE (44min) and, at the top of the trail, you'll see a *cortijo* (**6**) about 300m over to your right. The clear path continues through an area of gorse and rocks, crosses the **Puerto de Don Fernando** (**7**; 1h05min) and goes through a GAP IN A WALL. Carry on on across a grassy meadow. Looking to your left, you will see the *salto*, your goal, through a gap in the sierra. Access is through a gap in the wall, where a rocky path takes you down to the **Salto del Cabrero** (**8**; 1h19min). Return the same way.

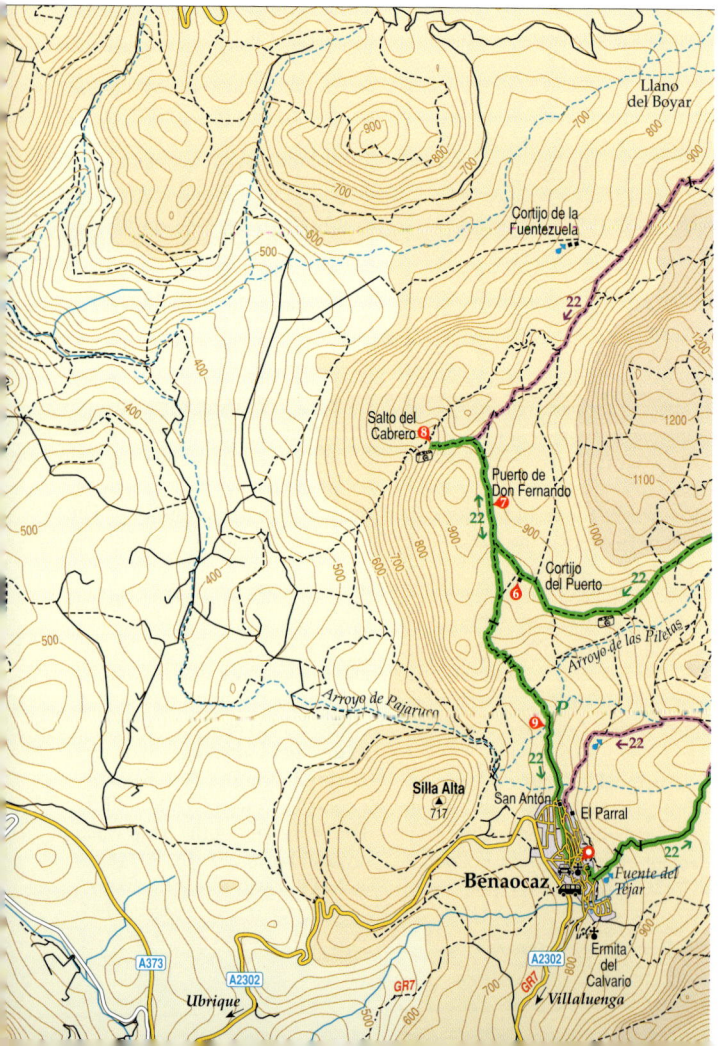

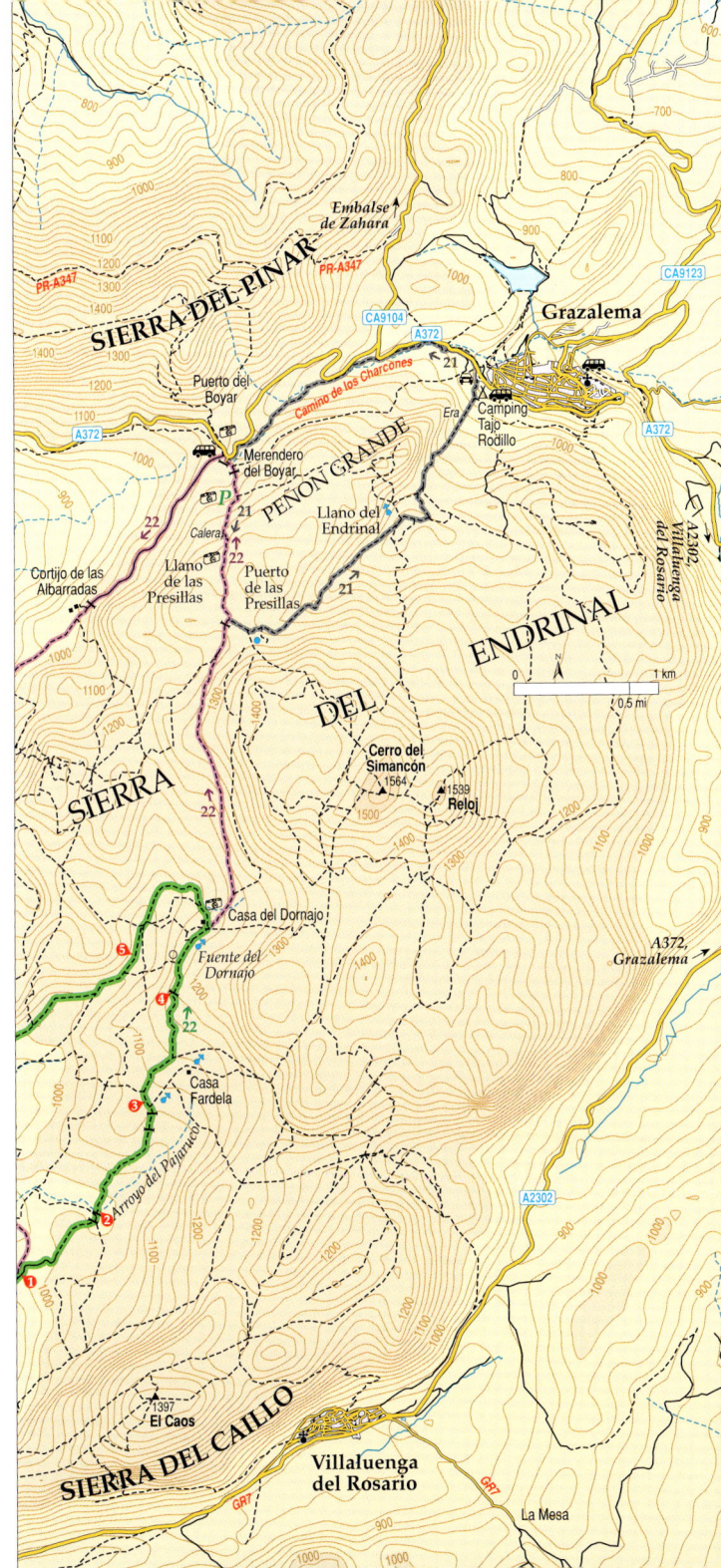

134 Landscapes of Andalucía

Alternative walks
1 From Benaocaz to Grazalema (11.5km/7.1mi; 3h48min). ● Strenuous, with an ascent of 550m/1800ft and descent of 470m/1540ft. Equipment as for main walk. Access: Plan this as either a morning or afternoon walk. If you walk in the morning, park in Benaocaz and return from Grazalema on the lunchtime 🚐 (Timetable 10). If you walk in the afternoon, park in Grazalema and take the lunchtime 🚐 from there to Benaocaz (Timetable 10) to start the walk. Follow *Alternative walk 2* (page 137) to the **Puerto de las Presillas** (2h30min), where a signpost points to Grazalema. Then pick up *Walk 21* at **❹** (with a map on page 130) and follow it to Grazalema.

2 Original route via the Puerto del Boyar (16.7km/10.4mi; 6h20min). ● Strenuous, with an ascent of 550m/1800ft and descent of 470m/1540ft. See page 137 for a description.

R uins of old farms, mountain passes and a geological rarity are just a few features of interest on this classic walk much loved by the local people, who hope that an agreement will be reached between the owners of the Albarradas *cortijo* and the powers that be, so that the route can once more be followed in its entirety. Cattle roam across much of the terrain, so you'll encounter an unusual number of gates and drystone walls built from the rocks which are strewn in abundance over the grassy surface of the whole region.

Start out from the CHURCH in **Benaocaz**: with your back to its tower (**O**), walk along Plaza de la Iglesia to Plaza del Cantillo on the left. Cross this square diagonally and take the steps up Calle Boabdil to a T-junction with a cobbled trail where you turn right (**3min**). The trail climbs gradually between smallholdings, running parallel with the Sierra del Caillo ridge which stretches into the distance on the right. You pass the **Fuente del Tejar** on the right (its trough is actually a Roman sarcophagus). The track is wide here, and easy going. Go through a first GATE (**10min**) onto open slopes. The trail bends right and upwards, soon passing through a METAL GATE. As it narrows and becomes a clear path, follow it up the valley between gorse and olive trees.

Pass between large rocks to an open area with a GATE IN THE WALL (**❶**; **28min**) diagonally to the right. Walk through the gate, now on a wider path. *(But for Short walk 1, go left without passing through the gate.)* Pitted from the constant pounding of cattle hooves, the ground is considerably eroded, but delicate little wildflowers still manage to survive in profusion.

Some stone ANIMAL PENS are tucked in at the foot of the rocky slope on the left (**41min**), before the path bears right into a dip. Pass through TWO GATES, the first a Heath Robinson affair, the second a rather more substantial one which opens into a stream, the **Arroyo del Pajaruco** (**❷**; **43min**). Cross the stream and head slightly left and up through more olive trees and gorse, the path becoming rocky and clearer as you proceed.

Right: Casa Fardela (ruins)

Ermita del Calvario at the southern end of Benaocaz

Pass through a GAP IN A WALL (**54min**) and follow the path to the left. The Sierra del Caillo ridge, rugged and barren, is in stark contrast to the delightful valley it protects. Soon coming into view ahead is a man-made structure, the *fuente* which serves Casa Fardela, a little way beyond it. The land round the house is fenced off so, about 50 metres before the *fuente*, go through the GATE in the fence on the left (**❸**; **1h04min**). You can just see the **Casa Fardela** ruins from here. Go up the grassy slope and veer right, to pick up a fairly clear path which takes you round the boundary and heads back towards the ridge (look out here for vultures soaring above you). From a little GULLY (**1h15min**) an animal trough can be seen about 50 metres ahead, and Casa Fardela is down to the right, now just out of sight beyond the wall. From the gully turn sharp left noticing, about 200 metres ahead, a conical mass of limestone with a sheer and jagged rock 'wall' stretching to its left and just visible above the trees. Strike out through rocks and trees — there's no real path, just animal trails — heading northwest and making for the end of the rock 'wall' *furthest to the left*. As you get closer, you'll pick up a clear path which takes you through a GATE (**❹**; **1h24min**) to the other side of the 'wall'.

From here your clear path bears right, circling round the slopes and gradually descending. When it appears to end, just carry on across rocks, to pick it up again as it continues round and descends past the **Fuente del Dornajo** and some stone-walled *corales*, animal enclosures (**1h30min**). Beyond these lie the substantial ruins of an old farm, the **Casa del Dornajo**, magnificently situated before a backdrop of the twin peaks of Simancón and Reloj. About 100m east of the ruins is a ancient *quejigo* written up in a catalogue of Andalucía's 'special' trees: its moss-covered roots are totally visible, since the ground on which it stands has eroded over centuries

Behind the house, scout around for a little-used path that descends in a northwesterly direction initially, into a little valley with huge holm oaks. The path descends through a GAP IN A WALL (**❺**; **1h45min**) and continues gently down with the Arroyo de las Piletas lower down on the left. This is a wonderland of more huge holm oaks and fantastic rock formations.

The path slowly rotates to the right and you rise to a 'natural' *mirador*, with views to Benaocaz and the Sierra del Caillo. Then the path rotates again, this time in a northwesterly direction. You pass a lived-in *cortijo* (**❻**; **2h40** on the left and its *algibe* (Arab water tank) a few paces on. Then you come to a wide, clear path at a T-junction: it's the path to the Puerto del Boyar. Turn right, to the **Puerto de Don Fernando** (❼; **2h55min**), a grassy flat expanse named for King Fernando who supposedly camped out there in the last phase of his Granada War.

From here head north to a signpost for the 'Vista Panorámica' from the **Salto del Cabrero** (❽; **3h15min**) — a gash in the vertical rock walls 80m (almost 300ft) high by 50m wide. The path takes you almost too close for comfort. Take in this amazing natural phenomenon, picking your vantage point and being careful of the sheer drops. One legend has it that a shepherd with a sick child jumped the crevice seeking help; there are of course other legends, some of them rather less positive.

Now you have a clear, signposted path to Benaocaz via the Puerto de Don Fernando and the *cortijo* and *aljibe* (now on your left; **5h25min**). Twice a day the goats are milked up here, and the churns filled and carried back by convoys of donkeys and mules to the villages. You cross a a tiny stone bridge across the bubbling **Arroyo del Pajaruco** (❾; **4h15min**; *P*22).

A cobbled trail takes you through a GATE and past the first of the worksheds and houses on the outskirts of **Benaocaz**. Pass an INFO BOARD for the start of the direct route to the Salto and walk along the main street of the village to the CHURCH (**4h35min**).

Original route via the Puerto del Boyar (in case it ever reopens)
Follow the main walk to **Casa del Dornajo**. Just before reaching the house (**1h35min**), look across to the left and locate the grassy tree-covered *collado* you'll be walking alongside later. Have a break and take some time to explore here.

Your onward route passes to the right of the HOUSE, heading northeast. Look for a CAIRN (**1h39min**) which signals your continuing path. It is rocky and initially follows the same direction, but it soon veers left and circles round the rocky slopes, with welcome shade provided by occasional evergreeen oaks. Steadily gaining altitude, you pass through a GAP IN A WALL (**2h06min**). The path goes straight ahead, then bears right to descend, steeply in places, along the side of the *collado* previously located. Go up through the GATE IN THE WALL at the head of the *collado* (**2h25min**) and carry straight on, heading north, on an indistinct path across the **Puerto de las Presillas** (**2h30min**). *(Signposts mark the start of a path which takes Alternative walk 1 and Walk 21 down to Grazalema.)*

The original route continues straight ahead. As the vegetation increases, the path becomes clearer and pebbly, and you start descending (**2h40min**). Down below, a valley opens out, and you'll see the road running through the Puerto del Boyar, a pass at 1103m. Wind steeply down to the valley floor and follow the path as it bears right, through a level stretch of pines and rocks (**2h51min**; *P*21).

At the far end, where the earth is churned up with animal tracks, the path turns left and becomes rocky as it descends, steeply at first, to reach a gully. You'll see the beginnings of the Río Guadalete here and the GATE ahead takes you out to the road at the *merendero,* stone picnic shelter, a little below the layby at the **Puerto del Boyar** (**3h**).

Walk a few metres up the wide path past the *merendero,* then go through a GATE signposted for the Salto del Cabrero. From here, a track takes you through pines, with views into the Llano del Boyar, a deep valley to the right. After you go through another GATE (**3h08min**), the Salto del Cabrero (Goatherd's Leap) is clearly visible ahead, but still a long way off. In the immediate distance lies a working *cortijo,* the **Cortijo de las Albarradas**. Just before you reach it, ARROWS (**3h26min**) direct you left off the track and lead you through a GATE alongside animal pens. The path, with a few markings at first, takes you through the middle of a narrow green valley. The trees attract many birds, and you'll hardly fail to catch a flash of colour as a redstart flies across your path.

The slope begins to drop away on the right, and the path runs along the foot of the steep rocky slopes on the left, descending a little (**3h46min**) to meet a FENCE. There's no way through the fence at this point, so the path veers right and through a GATE a little further downhill, before returning to run close to the cliffs again. Descend gradually through glorious woodland and cross a WATERCOURSE (**4h01min**), which could be torrential or dry depending on the season. Head uphill, to pass through another GATEWAY (**4h09min**). The main trail forks left here (as indicated by a waypost), but if the surrounds of the *cortijo* are not fenced off, first go *right* and cross a little grassy clearing. Poking out from amongst the rocks ahead is the chimney of the **Cortijo de la Fuentezuela** and just beyond the little house is its *fuente* (**4h13min**).

If you visit the *fuente,* leave it by turning up left on a steep clear narrow path which takes you on to a plateau where goats and cattle roam and rocks have been gathered into heaps to ensure sufficient grazing (**4h26min**). Vultures patrol the ridge to the left, so keep your eyes open as you follow the path past a RUIN and to a WALL (**4h35min**). Cross the wall and follow it downhill to the right. At the end, pick up a path going left, which leads to a GATE (**4h39min**).

Pass through yet another area of rocks and gorse, noticing a meadow down to the right. Beyond it, through a gap in the sierra, you'll see the valley below. Soon (**4h41min**) head off right through rocks and gorse down to the meadow — there isn't a clear path, but it doesn't matter. Cross the meadow and go through a GAP IN A WALL, where a rocky path descends straight ahead. The path takes you just alongside the **Salto del Cabrero** (**5h**), which opens up on the right — almost too close for comfort. Take in this amazing natural phenomenon, picking your vantage point and being careful of the sheer drops.

From here follow the main walk on page 137 to Benaocaz, adding just under two hours to all times — you reach the village in **6h20min**.

Walk 23: RIO MAJACEITE

See also photo on page 46
Distance: 8.7km/5.4mi; 2h55min
Grade: ● an easy out-and-back walk, signposted and waymarked green/white (SL-A116). Descent/ascent of 140m/460ft; but if you add in the visit to the Botanical gardens in El Bosque, reckon on 10.7km/6.6mi, with an additional ascent of 80m/260ft
Equipment: see page 51.
How to get there and return: 🚗 to/from the 75km-point on Car tour 7. Turn left and drive about half a kilometre down the tree-lined road towards Benamahoma. Park beside the bus stop, just by the roundabout at the entrance to the village (36° 45.956'N, 5°28.167'W). Except on Sundays/holidays, it is possible to catch the afternoon bus from El Bosque back to Benamahoma if you do not wish to walk both ways (🚌 Timetable 11).

Lose yourself in the beauty and freshness of the shady woodland canopy as you follow this typical riverside path downstream, then back again. It is often ablaze with wildflowers and, in the trees, you will hear nightingales, tits, warblers and woodpeckers. Dippers prefer to perch on rocks in the fast-flowing water, home to trout, otters and other aquatic creatures. In former times the power of the water was harnessed by several woollen mills, now in ruins. This walk can be enjoyed at any time of the year and, combined with a leisurely lunch in El Bosque, makes a perfect day out.

The walk starts by the BRIDGE in **Benamahoma** (○), just a few metres from the bus stop/car park. A tattered INFO PANEL provides some detail and a 'Río Majaceite' sign directs you left. Cross a stream and reach the path beside the **Río Majaceite**, immediately losing the sounds of habitation for the song of birds. Cross two little footbridges over streams but ignore one tucked away to the right which crosses the river. Pass below the FIRST OF THE RUINED MILLS (❶; **10min**) and, shortly afterwards, a long flat grassy area with another MILL up on the bank provides a good spot for a pause (❷; **14min**; *P*23). Beyond more ruins (**21min**), pass a bridge and keep straight on (WAYMARKING POST).

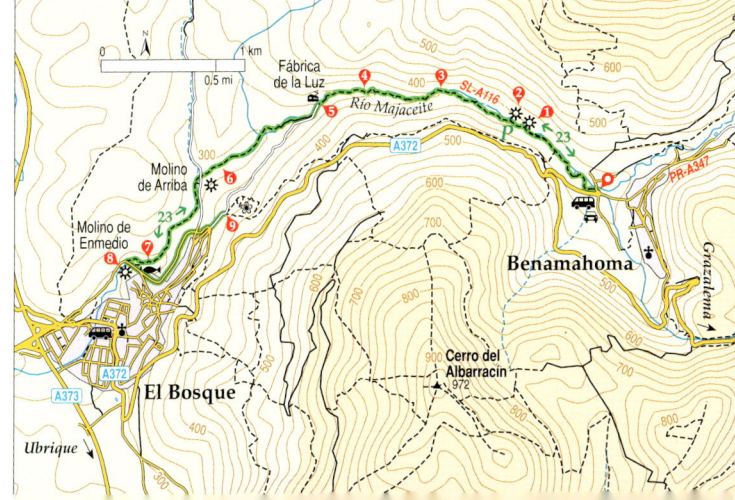

Landscape near Benamahoma

When several narrow paths fan out, keep to the highest and, as the banks close in, the main path becomes quite rocky and undulating for a while. You pass some CASCADES AND A POOL (❸; **31min**) before reaching the FIRST BRIDGE of several which take the path back and forth across the river. An *acequia* is just visible above a rock fall, shortly before a three-section bridge across an attractive open area of shallow WATERFALLS AND POOLS (**41min**). The next stretch used to be tricky, where you have to climb NARROW STEPS HEWN OUT OF THE ROCK (❹) about a metre above the river, but now — as elsewhere on the walk — there are sturdy handrails.

Soon the *fábrica de la luz* (hydroelectric plant) comes into sight on the opposite bank (❺; **51min**). It used to be served by the *acequia,* but ceased operating in 1963. A track leads away from here, into El Bosque, but you fork down right after just a few metres, to a path by the waterside. You cross the river again (**56min**), this time to a cultivated meadow with eucalyptus trees beyond it. After a pleasant level stroll along its edge you'll join a BOARDWALK and see across the river the partially renovated **Molino de Arriba** (❻; Upper Mill; **1h08min**).

The path crosses a wide TRACK (**1h11min**) and then a little BRIDGE over a stream. Soon El Bosque comes into view (**1h18min**). You pass some market gardens just before the large TROUT HATCHERY (❼; **1h25min**) which sits below the village. A small bridge takes you to its boundary fence to allow a closer look. Continue to the ROAD (**1h28min**) and cross a bridge to the **Molino de Enmedio** (❽; Middle Mill); this has been converted into a youth hostel. A convenient restaurant, not surprisingly, offers trout as its speciality.

The walk turns back here, but it's worth tackling the very steep slope up to the BOTANICAL GARDEN in village of **El Bosque**. The bus station, unfortunately, is located in the main square at the other end of the village, but returning along the riverside to your car at **Benamahoma** (**2h55min**) is just as pleasant as the outward walk.

BUS AND TRAIN TIMETABLES

TRAINS
1 Málaga — Torremolinos — Benalmádena — Fuengirola
An efficient train service leaves central Málaga (near the big department store El Corte Inglés) every half-hour. Timetables can be found at www.renfe.es (English pages).
Journey time Málaga—Fuengirola: about 42 minutes

BUSES
2 Marbella — Fuengirola — Torremolinos — Málaga (along the coast)
Regular bus service, approximately half-hourly to hourly (depending on time of day), including Sundays. Timetables at www.avanzabus.com (English pages)
Journey time Marbella—Málaga about 1h25min

3a Málaga — Torre del Mar — Nerja — Nerja (Cuevas) (along the coast) *(for Walks 10 and 11)*
Regular bus service, approximately hourly (depending on time of day), including Sundays. Timetables at www.alsa.es (English pages)
Journey time Málaga—Nerja about 1h30min

3b Nerja — Cueva de Nerja *(for Walk 10)*
Same bus as (3a) above. Buses depart from the ALSA kiosk just west of the Plaza Cantarero roundabout on Avda Ciudad de Pescia (the main road through Nerja). *Journey time from Nerja to the Cueva de Nerja about 10-15min*
Departs Nerja 08.30 09.40 10.40 11.30 12.25 13.10 13.30 14.30 14.55 15.55 16.40 17.30 20.00 21.40
Departs Cuevas 08.50 09.30 11.00 12.00 12.45 13.30 14.45 16.15 17.00 18.00 18.35 19.30 21.05

4 Órgiva — Pampaneira — Capileira *(for Walks 4 and 5)*
Buses are supposed to call at Carataunas and Soportújar but be aware that they sometimes don't bother. If you wish to get off at one of these villages make it clear to the driver. Timetables at www.alsa.es (English pages)

Órgiva	11.15	13.30	18.00	Capileira	07.00 16.45 18.15
Carataunas	11.25	13.40	18.10	Bubión	07.05 16.50 18.20
Soportújar	11.35	13.50	18.20	Pampaneira	07.10 16.55 18.25
Pampaneira	11.50	14.05	18.35	Soportújar	07.25 17.10 18.40
Bubión	12.00	14.15	18.45	Carataunas	07.30 17.15 18.45
Capileira	12.10	14.25	18.55	Órgiva	07.45 17.30 19.15

5 Frigiliana — Nerja *(for Walk 11); about 9 buses daily Mon-Sat, 7 on Sundays and holidays.* See timetables at www.andalucia.com/province/malaga/frigiliana/bus-service (English pages)
Departs Frigiliana (Mon-Sat): 07.00 08.00 10.10 10.50 11.40 12.45 14.00 15.30 16.30 17.35 19.30 21.00 22.00 (July and August); (Sun/holidays): 09.50 12.20 13.30 17.00 18.00 20.30 21.10
Departs Nerja bus station (Mon-Sat): 07.20 09.45 10.30 11.10 12.10 13.30 15.15 16.0017.10 19.00 20.30 21.30 (July and August)
(Sun/holidays): 09.30 12.00 13.00 16.15 17.30 20.00 20.50

142　Landscapes of Andalucía

6 Torre del Mar — Puente Don Manuel — Ventas de Zafarraya
(for Walk 13)
Departs Torre del Mar 08.00, 11.20; passes Puente Don Manuel 08.30, 12.10
Departs Puente Don Manuel 16.45
Timetables at www.alsa.es (English pages)

7 Fuengirola — Mijas *(for Walks 15 and 16)*
M-122 bus daily (08.00 to 22.00) in either direction, approximately every half hour. Timetables at www.siu.ctmam.ctan.es (English pages)
Journey time 20 minutes

8 Ojén — Marbella *(for Walk 17)*
Mon-Sat: Departs Ojén 07.15, 08.00 (Sat only), 08.45 (Sat only), 10.15, 13.10, 14.00, 16.00, 17.10, 20.25, 21.00
Departs Marbella (bus station) 07.50 (08.45 Sat only), 11.00, 13.00, 13.40, 15.00, 16.35, 18.15, 20.00 (not Sat), 21.00 (not Sat)
Sun/holidays: Departs Ojén 09.45, 13.15, 16.00, 20.15
Departs Marbella (bus station) 11.00, 13.45, 18.15, 21.00
Timetables at www.avanzabus. com (English pages)

9 Marbella — Istán *(for Walk 18) — no service Sat/Sun or holidays*
Autocares Transandalucia, from Avda Ricardo Soriano, Edificio Maria II (a couple of blocks east of McDonald's); timetables at www.istan.es; search 'Transport'. *Journey time 45 minutes*
Departs Marbella: 08.30, 15.15, 19.00
Departs Istán: 09.15, 16.00, 19.45

10 Ronda — Grazalema — Benaocaz — Ubrique:
Timetables at www.andalucistasdeubrique.com *(not in English)*: *horarios* = timetables, *invierno* = winter, *verano* = summer
(for Walks 21 and 22)

	Daily	
Ronda	12.30	18.15
Grazalema	13.00	18.45
Benaocaz	13.20	19.05
Ubrique	13.30	19.15

11 El Bosque — Benamahoma — Puerto del Boyar — Grazalema:
Timetables at www.andalucistasdeubrique.com *(not in English)*: *horarios* = timetables, *invierno* = winter, *verano* = summer
(for Walk 23); no service on Sat/Sun or holidays

	Mon-Fri	
El Bosque	06.45	15.15
Benamahoma	06.50	15.20
Puerto del Boyar	07.05	15.35
Grazalema	07.15	15.45
Grazalema	05.30	19.00
Puerto del Boyar	05.35	19.05
Benamahoma	05.50	19.20
El Bosque	06.00	19.30

 Index

Geographical names comprise the only entries in this index; for other subjects, see Contents on page 3. **Bold face** type indicates a photograph; *italic type* indicates a map (both may be in addition to other entries on the same page). (TT) = timetables for public transport; see pages 141-142.

Agrón 22
Alayos de Dilar 78-9, 82, **83**
Alhambra 22, **22-3**
Almuñécar 16, 20, 21, 23
Alozaina 41
Alpujarra 16-20, 53-70
Antequera **33**
Armilla 22
Arroyo
  de Huenes 23, *78-9*, 84
  de la Cueva de Melero 94
  de la Fuensanta 11, *120-1*
  de las Colmenas 108, 109, *110*
  del Laurel 108, *110*
  del Pajaruco 11, *130-1*, 133, 138
Atalbeitar 53, 55, 56
Axarquía 27-31, 85-98
Baños de Panjuila 53, 55
Barranco
  de la Coladilla 85, 86, *88-9*, 93
  de los Tejos *72-3*, 75, 76
  de San Juan 71, *72-3*
  del Búho 77, *78-9*, 80, 84
Bayacas 10, **17**, *68-69*, 70
Benalmádena 35, 37, 141 (TT)
Benamahoma 11, 45, *139*, **140**, 142 (TT)
Benaocaz 11, 44, *130-1*, 132, 133, 134, **136**, 138, 142 (TT)
Boca de la Pesca 77, *78-9*, **80**, 81, 82
Boquete de Zafarraya 30, 96, *97*, **98-9**
Bubión 18, 59, 65, 66, 67, 141 (TT)
Busquístar 9, **19**, 53, 55, **54-5**, 56
Caminito del Rey 101, *102*, **103**, **cover**
Camino
  de la Cuesta del Cielo 86, *88-9*
  de la Estrella 26, 71, *72-3*, 74
  de las Minas 86, *88-9*
  de las Nieves *124-5*, 126, **127**
  Real de Granada *97*, 100
Cañada del Cuerno **6-7**, *124-5*, 127
Canal de la Espartera 77, *78-9*, **80**, 82
Canillas de Albaida 10, 29, *94*
Capileira 9, **12**, 18, 57, **58**, *59*, 60, 61, **64**, 65, **66**, 67, 141 (TT)
Carataunas **17**, *68-9*, 70, 141 (TT)
Carihuelas **50**, 55, 55
Carratraca 34
Casa de Prado Redondo *72-3*, 75, 76

Casa Fardela *130-1*, 132, **135**
Casabermeja 32
Cerro de las Pipas *78-9*, 81, 82, **84**
Cerro Nicolás **112**, *112*
Churriana 34
Collado
  de las Sabinas *72-3*, 75, 76
  de los Apretaderos 85, *88-9*, 93
  de Trevenque 77, *78-9*
Cómpeta 29
Conejeras 13
Cortijo de Buena Vista *94*, **95**
Cortijos
  de la Civila 85, 87, *88-9*
  de Panjuila 9, 20, 55, 55
Cueva de Melero *94*
El Bosque 45, *139*, 140, 142 (TT)
El Burgo 11, 40, 119, *120-1*, 122
El Chorro Nature Reserve 10, 33-4, **101**, *102*, **103**
El Desvío 25
El Dornajo *see* Sierra Nevada
El Nacimiento 11, **115**, 117, **118**
El Pinarillo 85, **86**, *88-9*
El Tajo 11, 117
El Torcal **13**, 33
Embalse
  de los Bermejales 12, 22
  de Viñuela 12, 27
  de Zahara **43**, 44
Entrerrios 36, 108, *110*, 142 (TT)
Ermita
  de Santa Ana 29, *94*
  del Calvario (Mijas) 15, 36, **36-7**, 104, 105, *106*; (Benaocaz) *132*, **136**
Espino 96, *97*, **98-99**
Estación de San Juan 10, 26, 71, *72-3*, 74
Ferreirola 53, 55, **55**
Frigiliana 27, **29**, *88-9*, 90, 91, **92**, 93, 141 (TT)
Fuengirola 37, 141 (TT), 142 (TT)
Fuente
  Agria 12, 16, 18, 55, 56
  del Esparto 85, *88-9*
  del Hervidero 23, 77, *78-9*, 80, 81, 82, 84
Granada 22, **22-3**

143

Grazalema 45, 46, 128, *130-1*, **132**, 133, 134, 142 (TT)
Güéjar Sierra 26, 71
Istán 11, 38, 42, *115*, **116**, 117, **118**, 142 (TT)
Jayena 22
Juanar 11, 111, *112*, 114
Jete 23
La Cebadilla *59*, 60, 61, *65*
La Fuensanta 11, 40, 119, *120-1*
La Molineta 27, *88-9*, **90**, 91, **93**
La Poza 12, 18
La Rahije 12, 27
La Zubia 21, 24
Las Gabias 22
Maitena Visitor Centre 26, 71, *72-3*, 74, 76
Málaga 141 (TT)
Malaha 22
Marbella 10, 38, 42, 111, *112*, 141 (TT), 142 (TT)
Maro *88-9*
Mijas 10, 35, **37**, **104**, 105, *106*, 107, 141 (TT)
Monda 41
Mulhacén **20**, 60, 63-4, **74**
Nerja 27, **30**, *88-9*, 90, 93, 141 (TT)
Cueva de Nerja 27, 31, 85-6, *88-9*, 90, 93, 141 (TT)
Ojén 42, 111, *112*, 114, 142 (TT)
Órgiva 17, 66, 67, *68-9*, **70**, 141 (TT)
Otívar 23
Pampaneira 12, **15**, 18, *59*, *65*, 66, 67, *68-9*, 141 (TT)
Parque Natural
de Ardales 33
Montes de Málaga 32
Sierra de las Nieves 13, 39, 123, *124-5*, 126
Torcal de Antequera **13**, 32-3
Peñón
de los Enamorados 123, *124-5*
Grande **129**, *130-1*, **132**
Pitres 18, *55*
Pórtugos 12, 18, *55*
Prado Llano **25**, 26
Puente de Aguila 27
Puente de los Siete Ojos 10, 24, 77, *78-9*,
Puente Don Manuel 30, 96, *97*, 100, 141 (TT)
Puerto
de los Pilones 123, *124-5*, 127
de Marbella 111, *112*, 114
del Boyar 11, 46, *130-1*, 133, 137, 142 (TT)
Quejigales 123, *124-5*, 127
Río
Alaminos 36, 37, 108, *110*

Río *(continued)*
Alcaucín 96, *97*, 98
Chico 17, *68-9*, 70
Chillar 27, *88-9*, 90, 91, 92
del Burgo 11, **41**, 119, *120-1*, **122**
Dilar *78-9*, 81, *82*, **83**
Fuengirola 36, 37
Genil 26, 71, *72-3*, **74**, 76
Guadalete 11, 44, 46, 128, *130-1*
Guadalfeo 16, 20, 21
Guadalhorce *102*, **103**
Guadalmedina 32
Guarnón *72-3*, **74**
Higuerón *88-9*, 91-3
Majaceite 11, **46**, *139*
Naute *59*, 60, *62*, *65*
Poqueira 9, 12, 17, **57**, *59*, 60, *62*, *65*
Sanguino 87, *88-9*
Seco *72-3*, 75,
Trevélez 12, **19**, 53, *55*
Verde 42, *115*, 118
Ronda **38-9**, 43, 46, 142 (TT)
Salares 30, 31
Salobreña 16, 21
Salto del Cabrero 45, *130-1*, **132**, **133**, 138
San Pedro 38
Sierra
Blanca 111, *115*, 117
de Grazalema 6, 7, 39, 43-46, **128**-140
de las Nieves **6-7**, 13, 38-42, 111-123, *124-5*, 126-7
de Mijas 10, 35, 36, **37**, *106*
del Caillo *130-1*, **132**, 134, **135**
del Endrinal *130-1*
del Pinar *130-1*
Nevada 12, 18, 21-26, 71-84; Visitor Centre (El Dornajo) 21, 24, 25, *72-3*
Soportújar *68-9*, 141 (TT)
Torre del Mar 31, 141 (TT)
Torremolinos 32, 34, 141 (TT)
Torrox 29
Torrox Costa 31
Torvizcón 20
Trevélez 12, **19**
Trevenque 10, 24, *78-9*
Ubrique 44, 142 (TT)
Vega de Granada **4-5**, 21
Veleta **2**, **25**, **62-3**, **68**
Vélez de Benaudalla 20
Vélez Málaga 31
Ventas de Zafarraya 96, *97*, 98, 141 (TT)
Villaluenga del Rosario 44, *130-1*, *132*
Villanueva 32
Viñuela 12
Yunquera 40